Turkey

A SHORT HİSTORY

turquie
grece
grece
le siege du grant turc auec .ij. de ses pncipaulx cōseilles
le siege du capiteine gnal de la turquie

Turkey

A SHORT HİSTORY

Norman Stone

For Canon Ian Sherwood,
Chaplain of the Crimean Memorial Church, Istanbul

First published in the United Kingdom in 2010 by
Thames & Hudson Ltd, 181A High Holborn,
London WC1V 7QX

First paperback edition 2012
Reprinted 2014

British Library Cataloguing-in-Publication Data
A catalogue record for this book is available from the British Library
ISBN 978-0-500-29038-5

Printed in China by Toppan Leefung

CONTENTS

INTRODUCTION

Constantinople, capital city of the later Roman Empire, had a commanding position for the world's trade, because it had the best natural harbour between Europe and Asia. As such, it became the capital of a successor-empire, the Ottoman, or Turkish, in 1453, and the city's commanding position is still very obvious. As I write this book, in a flat overlooking the Bosphorus, I can see up to a hundred ships passing through every day, some of them huge tankers or container ships from China, making their way to or from the Black Sea. Relics of Istanbul's imperial past are all around – whether the Great Church of Christian Rome, the sixth-century Aya Sofya (Hagia Sophia), or the imposing mosques constructed by the Turkish Sultans.

The Ottoman Empire is a spectre haunting the modern world. It vanished from the map at the end of the First World War, and the vast area that it once controlled has seen one problem after another. From the fourteenth century onwards, it had expanded from a base in what is now north-western Turkey, and it became a world empire, stretching from the Atlantic coast of Morocco to the river Volga in Russia, and from the present Austro-Hungarian border to Yemen and even Ethiopia. In the eighteenth century the empire lost its primacy of the Black Sea and the Caucasus to Russia; in the nineteenth it lost the Balkans to nation states, of which Greece was the most prominent; in the twentieth, it lost Arab lands. The Balkans and the Middle East have presented problems to the world ever since then, and so, nowadays, there is a certain nostalgia for the Ottoman Empire.

The Englishman, 'Lawrence of Arabia', who had done much in 1916 to encourage an Arab revolt against the Turks – foreigners called them that, though they themselves used the word only later – looked at Iraq, as the British took it over in 1919, and wondered why the place had fallen into a murderous conflict of all against all: the British had an army of 100,000, complete with tanks, aircraft and poison gas, whereas the Turks had kept the peace in their three Iraqi provinces of Basra, Mosul and Baghdad with 14,000 locally raised men and only 200 executions per annum. The same remark might be passed about Palestine, where the British, after thirty years spent trying to get Jews and Arabs to agree, finally just threw in their hand and let the United Nations take over. The Balkans (or for that matter the Caucasus) show another version of the same conundrum. The Ottoman Empire had kept the peace, or at any rate had kept a lid on problems, and this compares quite well with, say, British India, which – though a viceroy in 1904 thought that it would go on 'for ever' – lasted less than a century.

British India also ended in partition, resulting in the creation of Pakistan as an Islamic state. It in turn was partitioned, as Bangladesh split off, and the world will not entirely be taken by surprise if Pakistan itself also splits, according to developments in Afghanistan. This opens a central question as regards modern Turkey. The record of Islam in state building, in modern times, has not been unspotted. We do not need to go as far as a young Turkish historian of Central Asia, Hasan Ali Karasar, and say 'Islam, politics, economics: choose two', but the question is valid enough. The Ottoman Empire and the Turkish Republic that succeeded it in Anatolia would have to be given serious consideration in the answer. To what extent was the success of the Ottomans based on Islam, or would you read this the other way round, and just say that the Ottomans were successful when their Islam was not taken too seriously?

Republican Turks were adamant that religion had to be taken out of the state, and they regarded it as a tremendous impediment to development. When they set up the Republic in 1923, their model was France, where

Church and State had been separated in 1905, and nuns had been expelled from convents at bayonet point. The Catholic Church had, on the whole, endorsed the persecution of the (wrongly) alleged Jewish spy, Alfred Dreyfus, and paid for this. But there was a long tradition of anti-clericalism in France, and stout Republicans argued that Catholicism was responsible for the country's decline, and for the nation being overtaken by England and Germany. There were Italians and Spaniards who thought along the same lines. Nowadays, Turkey is seeking membership of the European Union and if there is a country for her to consider as fraternal, it would be Spain: world empire, with seven centuries of Islam in the background, and then nation state with military rule never far from the surface. Turkey did not have a civil war like Spain's, but her experience in the First World War offers some dreadful parallels.

The makers of the Republic were hostile to the Ottoman inheritance, and in 1924 some hundred members of the dynasty were exiled abroad, with $2,000 each: the men were not allowed back until the 1970s. There is a line in Proust, to the effect that someone looks on history as would a newly born chicken at the bits of the eggshell from which it had been hatched. The Republicans had after all won the war of independence, the first real Turkish victory since the seventeenth century, and it had been a triumph born out of considerable adversity. The Sultan would have preferred to come to terms with the western Powers, and especially the British, as some sort of Aga Khan. The Republicans therefore repudiated him and his legacy. The Aya Sofya was turned into a museum, and the Islamists were ruthlessly bundled out of the university, to be replaced by a star cluster of refugees from Hitler's Germany, with which I have begun the book.

The Republic has been a considerable success, especially since 1980, when there was a military coup comparable with that of Pinochet in Chile, and as I write there are two world-class engineering projects going ahead. The first is tunnelling under the Bosphorus, which will bring fast trains from Ankara to Europe, in the manner of the Channel Tunnel. The second is greater still. Eastern Turkey has remained quite underdeveloped, except for odd areas. Now, large dams constructed over the biblical rivers, the Tigris and the Euphrates, are supplying not just irrigation and hydroelectricity, but something of a social revolution as well, because a new level of prosperity is lifting that (mainly Kurdish) area of Anatolia into a world altogether different from its neighbours to the east and south. However, the Republic has run into the problems that face all Enlightenments: the children eat the parents. The secularists have been displaced by Anatolians, often religious, and there has been much questioning as to the very identity of the Turks.

If you are Turkish, you have to ask what you owe to: (1) the ancient native Turkish tradition; (2) Persia; (3) Byzantium; (4) Islam; (5) what sort of Islam; and (6) conscious westernization. The none-too-happy saga of Turkey's application to join the European Union brings all this to the fore, and there has been another important change in the terms of the debate: that much of Turkey is now tolerably prosperous (in terms of economic weight, she is worth more than the ex-Communist member states of the European Union, and, again like Spain, has 'taken off' economically). The early managers of the Republic were out-and-out westernizers, with an ideological basis in Turkish nationalism and a determination to remove from public life the influence of a religion that could easily be dismissed as obscurantist. But the matter is not at all simple. Prosperity spread, and lifted off sleepy provincial towns in Anatolia. Their politics being religious, Turkey is governed, and not too badly governed either, by a government that sometimes cites European Christian Democracy as its exemplar. This has caused much convulsion, and nowadays there is an extraordinary concern for history: even taxi drivers know quite a lot about it.

It is not really for an outsider to comment, and I resolutely refrain from doing so, except to say that modern Turkey is undergoing a smudgy version of what happened in the later nineteenth century, under Sultan Abdülhamit II. I do not, of course, know the outcome. Abdülhamit himself is being re-examined. It is true that in his time there was much co-operation with the West while the empire remained religiously based (at least in theory). There was also education, and the emergence of the technical intelligentsia that has been so important for the making of the Republic. That technical intelligentsia and the army rebelled against Abdülhamit, and a version of that quarrel is still with us.

In the present book, I trace, I hope, the six factors outlined above that have gone into the making of Turkey today. They are all difficult even for a long-term resident foreigner such as myself, and Turkish friends, wittingly or unwittingly, have told me much. I cannot, and they will understand, make one of the long lists that would conventionally follow such a statement. I will only say that I have hugely enoyed teaching at Bilkent University, especially at the undergraduate level; have remained on friendly terms with some of my graduate students as we all grew older, and as I somehow managed to reach a level of Turkish at which taxi drivers shook their heads in bewilderment at my Scottish-accented Ottoman words; and I remember my weekly seminar on European History at Boğaziçi University with special affection. I have been fortunate to have two of those former students, Hasan Ali Karasar, now a Bilkent colleague, and Murat Siviloğlu, now at Peterhouse, Cambridge, read my manuscript, along with the veteran of Turkish history, Andrew Mango. Fahri Dikkaya at Bilkent has kept me from making gross misstatements as regards the early Ottomans, the archaeology of whom he knows. If mistakes got through it is because Homer nodded. It remains for me to thank the splendidly efficient team at Thames & Hudson, and my agent, Caroline Michel, for organizing this assignment, which has taught me much.

NOTE ON NOMENCLATURE

I firmly believe that historic names should be used in history books, and, of course, no offence is intended: thus 'Constantinople' and 'Smyrna' are used until the end of the empire, just as 'Aleppo' and 'Salonica' are standard. I have omitted diacriticals in Ottoman transcriptions. They make sense only if you can read the original.

PRELUDE

Fritz Neumark wrote one of the noblest books in the German language, his memoirs of Turkey, *Zuflucht am Bosporus* (Refuge on the Bosphorus). He is not a romantic, but he describes how, in the late summer of 1933, his ship arrived in Istanbul. In those days it was quite heavily green and wooded. You moved past the Blue Mosque, then the Aya Sofya and the Topkapı Palace, and you docked across the Golden Horn, an inlet of the Bosphorus, at Galata, dominated by a medieval Italian tower, of a type recognizable from Renaissance paintings. Kurdish porters humped your luggage up the street of steps, in Greek *Skalakia*, and you put up at the Park Hotel, an art deco wedding-cake of a building, next to the old German embassy. Shortly after his arrival, Neumark had to attend a reception given by the foreign minister; if you needed evening clothes, a Greek tailor ran them up in three days. A refugee from Hitler's Germany, he had found a post, teaching the principles of finance, at a new university in Istanbul. Roughly a thousand such Germans arrived in Turkey at this period, and for a time it seemed they would be headed by Albert Einstein, who had accepted the Chair of Theoretical Physics (although he did not in the end take it, because he was expected to teach and did not want to: he went to Princeton instead). However, the other Germans who came were remarkable enough, and for a decade or so the new Istanbul University had some claim to be the best in the world.

Economics was taught by Wilhelm Röpke, later architect of the post-war German economic miracle; the philosophy of mathematics by Hans Reichenbach, who also organized the Turkish ski team. The pride of the collection, in his way, was Hellmut Ritter, a very difficult, mean and twisted man, who was in German Intelligence in the First World War. He knew Arabic and Persian to the point at which he was an expert in mystic Islamic poetry, was expelled from the Orient Institute in Hamburg for homosexuality (given the date and place, the action must have been quite advanced), and went to Turkey, where at first he kept body and soul together by playing the cello in a string quartet at Ankara station. He then became librarian of Istanbul University, re-ordering a catalogue that had up until his time been kept by a little old man with a beard who squiggled entries on bits of paper and put them in a drawer.

The supporting cast of those Germans was also of very high quality, including Carl Ebert, founding artistic director of Glyndebourne opera, who established the opera and drama school of the Ankara Conservatory in 1936, and the composer Paul Hindemith, who helped reorganize musical education in Turkey. The star of them all is Ernst Reuter, later mayor of West Berlin at the time of the Soviet blockade and the airlift of 1948. He had been rescued from a concentration camp by English Quakers, and went to Ankara to teach town planning in 1935. His Turkish was such that he was put on the language-reform commission, the aim of which was to replace Arabic and Persian words by proper old Turkish ones, which Reuter was supposed to know as he had been a prisoner-of-war in Central Asia in 1917. He probably made them up. Otherwise he was remembered with much affection in Ankara, as a very tall man with a beret, riding around on an old-fashioned bicycle, his affairs much gossiped about. Ankara itself had been set up as the new capital by Central Europeans: Professor Hermann Jansen for the planning (clever) and Professor Clemens Holzmeister for the execution (also clever, but derailed).

Turkey needed these men because the country had been launched on a radical programme of cultural, economic and military westernization. The Turkey of today, a republic proclaimed in 1923, more or less with the present-day borders, was the heartland of the Ottoman Empire which, at its greatest extent, had run well into three continents. It had then suffered a decline and, with the First World War, a fall. Turkey emerged as the outcome of a national resistance, and her leaders were determined to do no more declining: there would be modernization. The greatest reform concerned language, in 1928. Turkish was written until then in an Arabic script and contained a large number of Arabic or, in matters to do with emotion or food, Persian words. However, Arabic is a guttural language, with only three vowels, while Turkish has eight, and there are even troubles as regards consonants, there being four versions in Arabic of 'z'. For Turkish, a Latin or even a Cyrillic alphabet made more sense, if your aim was to make the mass of the people literate. As often happens in Turkey, in this the army had been the creative force. In the First World War, if you needed to send a coded telegram, you had the original transliterated into French, then it was encoded and sent by Morse dots and dashes, after which it had to be unravelled at the other end. Officers were already suggesting that the whole process needed to be simplified and ten years after the war ended that was what happened: in a month, the alphabet was latinized.

In due course literacy did indeed spread, and Turkey today produces 11,000 translations from foreign languages every year, whereas in the Middle East the figure is 300. Turkish writers put themselves on the world's map quite early on, 'the Fisherman of Halicarnassus' was a bestselling author in England even in the 1940s, as Orhan Pamuk is today. But there were great drawbacks: huge parts of the literary tradition were lost; and in the old Imperial House of Applied Sciences – the official name of the university – scholars objected to the reform, dragged their feet. In 1932, the place was simply closed down, and this accounts for the arrival of so many foreigners. That Hitler had chased out so many of the best Germans was, in that sense, a bonus. But they were only the latest in quite a long line of foreigners. The outstanding Turkish poet of the twentieth century, Nazım Hikmet – himself the grandson of an exiled Pole – wrote a famous line about Turkey, and by extension the Turks' occupation of Anatolia: 'charging out of Asia, and stretching like a mare's head into the Mediterranean'.

ONE Origins

ORIGINS

The centrepiece of the Ottoman Empire was the Topkapı Palace, on the small peninsula that Fritz Neumark's ship rounded on its way to the dock in the harbour of the Golden Horn. It is a palace unlike any other: vast in acreage, but not in height. It is laid out in courtyards, with many pavilions, some of them very intricate, which are called *köşk* (the origin of our own word, 'kiosk'), and this reflected the rulers' own understanding of their origins. The palace is an elaborate version of the tented headquarters of a nomadic chieftain, and the Ottoman symbol was the horsetail: the more such standards outside the tent, the higher the rank; when the army was on the march, the tents were often tremendous works of art. The best display of them is in Cracow, where they were taken after the siege of Vienna in 1683.

The early Turks came from the Altai region in Central Asia, on the western border of present-day Mongolia, and may even have had some distant links across the straits to Alaska (the Eskimo word for 'bear' is the Turkish *ayı*). The first written reference to them is a Chinese *tyu-kyu* of the second century BC, a name that appears here and there, subsequently, in Chinese sources of the sixth century. It denoted nomadic warrior tribes, practised at raiding superior civilizations: the word 'Turk' was the name of the dominant tribe, and means 'strong man'. These nomads, related to the Mongols and perhaps also to the Huns, spread out over the vast tableland of Central Asia, and caused much trouble for the Chinese, sometimes establishing steppe empires that lasted for a generation or two before being absorbed by the more settled natives. Much of Chinese history is about these battles on the long, open frontier; the necessity for the Great Wall being a case in point. The steppe empire that really stood out was that of the Uyghurs, of around 800 AD, who took literacy and much else from the Chinese. There were dynasties with obvious Turkish antecedents, including that of the fabled Kublai Khan (Kubilay is a common enough first name in Turkey), who in 1272 established Hanbalık, 'city of the ruler', the modern-day Beijing.

Some of these Turkish connotations may be no more than romantic speculation. Does 'Kirghiz' mean in Turkish 'the forty-two' (tribes), or something else, such as 'nomad'? In the twelfth and thirteenth centuries, Marco Polo referred to Chinese Turkestan as 'Great Turkey', and the place names are obvious: the river Yenisei in Russia takes its name from *yeni çay* or 'new river'; and the earlier name of Stalingrad, Tsaritsyn, has nothing to do with 'Tsar' but comes from *sarı su*, 'yellow water'. There are some oddities. Tundra is *dondurma*, which nowadays means 'ice cream'. The linguistic descendants of old Turkish have, of course, grown in some cases far apart, although Anatolian Turks say they find Kirghiz quite easy, despite the thousands of miles in between. The grammar is regular, but different from English, in that prepositions, tenses and the like are added to the main word, with the vowel changing according to the main word's dominant vowel. This is maybe best illustrated by the word 'pastrami', one of none-too-many words that we owe to these old Turks. It is an Italian version of the original *pastırma*, nowadays sold as very thin slices of dried beef, preserved in a cake of spices, of which cumin (*çemen*) is chief. *Pas* is the stem of a verb meaning 'press'. *Tır* (the dotless *ı* pronounced something like a French 'eu' and marking a vowel change that is used after an 'a') indicated causation, and *ma* (also a vowel change: it could have been *me*) turns it all into a verbal noun or gerund. This foodstuff, kept under the saddle, maintained nomadic horse archers for hundreds of miles across the Central Asian steppe.

The earliest writing in Turkish (with a runic alphabet) dates from the eighth century, around Lake Baikal, and refers to *dokuz oğuz* 'nine tribes', but quite soon the Uyghur version of the language, written vertically in the Chinese manner, prevailed, and it was used in the diplomatic correspondence of the great Mongol conqueror, Genghis Khan (*c.* 1167–1227).[1]

Otherwise these early Turks do not leave a literary trace and you have to study them using outside sources – Chinese, Persian, Arab, Byzantine. They moved west and south-west, towards the great civilizations on the periphery of Central Asia. They came in waves, two of them of tidal proportions, as we shall see. Genghis Khan, in the early thirteenth century, led a federation of related Mongol and Turkish (or Tatar) tribes. He had a successor a century later, a wrecker of world proportions, Tamerlane (*c.* 1336–1405), of Turkish origin (*Timur* is a variant of the word meaning 'iron' and *lenk* means 'lame'). They and their descendants took over China, much of Russia, and India; 'Mughal', a version of 'Mongol', reflects this: in Turkish, Taj Mahal means 'crown quarter'; and the language of Pakistan, Urdu, is a variant of the word *ordu*, meaning 'army'. There is a famous French book on these matters, René Grousset's *L'empire des steppes* (1939), and there are Turkish connections all over the area, including Afghanistan, where you can often be understood if you use the language; but the important link, as far as the Anatolian Turks is concerned, is with Persia. This was, of course, the greatest historic civilization of the whole Middle East and there are controversies as to the Turks' relationship with it – controversies that involve not just cultural borrowings, but Islam itself.

As early as the eighth century, Turkish mercenaries had made their appearance in Persia, in the then capital of which, Baghdad, the Caliphate reigned over all Islam. Some had gone on to Syria or Egypt. However, the decisive moment came in the later tenth century, when one of the Oğuz (western Turks) tribes arrived on the Persian outskirts. Its chief was one

1 The letter *ğ* is not pronounced: it just lengthens the preceding vowel. Transcribing these Turkish sounds – as with *ı* – took a bit of thought, in the 1920s, and there was some help from the Hungarians, who had faced something of the same problem. Their *gy*, pronounced more or less as 'dj' in English but with more of a clack, is rendered as a *c* in Turkish.

Selçuk, meaning 'little flood' in Arabic and maybe something else in Turkish. The Turks brought a religious iconography that came from the world of Siberia: shamanism, with its own druids, the emblems being a peregrine and a hawk – *tuğrul* and *çağrı* – which are still used as first names. In 1055 they entered Baghdad and penetrated the state: at a great age, their leader, Tuğrul Bey, married the daughter of the Caliph in a ceremony under Turkish rites: as a French historian, Jean-Paul Roux, says, it was the equivalent of marrying an African chief to a Habsburg to the sound of tom-toms.

Then these Turks took over Persia altogether. To this day, the school textbooks reflect ancient quarrels or hard-luck stories. Little Greeks or Iranians learn that their ancestors, elegantly clad in white, discussed poetry in the subjunctive while dignified matrons beamed over gambolling sheep, and flaxen-haired maidens stirred the pot, all under clear skies, until, out of the blue, squat and hairy savages, offering rapine, arrived. These are the Turks, their oppression lasting for centuries. Little Turks on the other hand, learn that effete civilizations, eunuchs, etc., were given some sort of vigour by the arrival of their ancestors. When, in the 1930s, Turks were compelled to adopt names in the European manner, Cenk, Tusa (although that one is probably Balkan) and Savas, meaning 'battle', were quite popular, and Zafer, Galip, Mansur, Kazan, denoting 'victory', even more so. And there are many words for fighting in Turkish.

The main trick was for Turkish warriors to appear, and, as a military elite, take over an old-established state. They were extraordinarily adaptable and learned from the peoples whom they penetrated. In some, but not all, cases they took over the religion. In the case of the Mongols, this was Buddhism or a form of Christianity; but otherwise, in India or Persia, it was generally Islam, which at that time, around 1100, was the most civilized form of religion (as the buildings of Samarkand especially show). The Persians, heirs to one of the great civilizations of the world, got a Turkish aristocracy and to this day wonder why the Turks brought off first an empire and then a working modern state, whereas they did not (modern Turkey contains a million refugees from that region).

The most interesting synthesis is Russian. Napoleon famously said, scratch the Russian and you discover the Tatar. Russia in the thirteenth century succumbed, for two centuries, to the Mongols, or Tatars (originally, as with 'Turk' itself, just the name of a dominant tribe). A third of the old aristocracy had Tatar names: Yusupov (from 'Yusuf') or Muratov (from 'Murat'), and Ivan the Terrible himself was descended from Genghis Khan. The Tatars knew how to build up a state – reflected by the Russian words for 'handcuffs' and 'treasury'. The Russian princes eventually copied the Tatars, Moscow most successfully, and in 1552, Ivan the Terrible conquered the Tatar capital, Kazan, on the Volga. Nineteenth-century warhorses then presented Russian history as a sort of crusade in which indignant peasants freed themselves from 'the Tatar yoke'. But that phrase was first used only in 1571, when the Orthodox Church was trying to resist Ivan the Terrible, who used Tatars to build up a state that did not tolerate Orthodox pretentions. Before then, the relationship was a great deal more complicated, including intermarriage.

The Persian Turks were called 'Great Seljuks', but their lesser cousins, still in many cases nomadic, drove into Anatolia. Their chief, Alp Arslan (r. 1064–72), was really leading his horde (that word again comes from *ordu*) into Syria, a rich country. Along the way, his men were probing the eastern frontiers of Byzantium, the eastern Roman Empire, and upsetting Byzantium's clients, Christian states in the southern Caucasus, who looked to Constantinople. An emperor, Romanus Diogenes, foolishly decided to march an army all the way to the east. In 1071, there was a battle, at Manzikert, now Malazgirt, an undistinguished place on a high plateau north of Lake Van, and the Byzantines lost, severely weakening their hold on eastern and central Anatolia. Over the next two centuries, the Seljuk Turks established themselves in much, though not all, of Anatolia; Byzantium was confined to the area of Constantinople, parts of the Balkans, and a few coastal places.

The Seljuks left the Christian population of Anatolia alone. In Cappadocia, some four hours' drive east of Ankara, there are valleys where Christians lived undisturbed, building rock churches with frescoes that are now one of the world's tourist sites. The frescoes painted in the era of Byzantine revival, in the tenth and early eleventh centuries, have a magnificent quality, and one of them was taken to newly Christian Russia, as Our Lady of Vladimir. After the Seljuk conquest, the frescoes become crude, but they are evidence that the Turks developed a tolerant and law-abiding civilization. They were not interested in suppressing other people's religions, and in any case there were too few of them, with a Christian population all around. There was much intermarriage and trade instead. A Byzantine princess of literary disposition, Anna Comnena, said in the twelfth century that the inhabitants of Anatolia divided between Greeks, barbarians, and 'mixo-barbarians', meaning intermarried Turks.

The Seljuk capital, Konya (the old Roman Iconium), and a major city, Kayseri (the old Caesarea in Cappadocia), have some splendid architecture, in the style of the great places of Samarkand and Bukhara in Central Asia.[2] Grand mosques were constructed, to which schools, hospitals, and so forth were sometimes attached, as education was practised. But the early Turks were not very good at religious rules. They were more inclined to put up small prayer-houses than grand mosques, as more suited to their version of Islam, and their women went uncovered; wine was drunk; there was dancing, much to the scandal of a fourteenth-century Arab traveller, Ibn Battuta.

Eventually, Byzantium did collapse, but it happened from the west, not the east. There had always been rivalry between Rome and Constantinople, and it became worse, because the Pope, as Bishop of Rome, claimed to be the

2 On most of them there is a double-headed eagle. This became the crest both of Russia and Austria, and you might assume, not senselessly, that it was Byzantine in origin, and reflected the division of the Roman Empire, with its single eagle, into two, with Rome and Constantinople as capitals. Not so. There is an original in the splendid Ankara Museum of Anatolian Civilizations, and it is marked 'Hittite, 2000 BC'.

head of the entire Church, whereas Byzantium developed its own form of Christianity: Orthodoxy. Western – 'Latin' – Crusaders, a combination of Normans and Venetians, attacked Byzantium in 1204, and wrecked it. This was a decisive episode. Until then, the Byzantines had been ahead of the West in terms of technology, and western Europeans arrived in Constantinople as gawping provincials. The Byzantines had a formidable weapon, Greek fire, which meant pumping out a combustible mixture of oil that ignited and burned ships; with this, they had resisted several sieges. Now, in 1204, as members of what is known as the Fourth Crusade, the Venetians had worked out how to treat leather with chemicals, such that their ships and siege-towers were invulnerable. They got over the great wall, built by the emperor Theodosius in the fifth century, and ransacked the city. The great Pantocrator church, where the Comneni emperors were buried (it is now Zeyrek Mosque) was stripped of the tombs, and today the only sign of their existence is a tiny sliver of gold too high in the wall to have been removed. For the next two centuries, Byzantium was under the Latins, and although she recovered, she had been broken. She was really run by Venetians and Genoese, fighting each other for the trade of the Black Sea (the Turkish coast of which is still studded with the ruins of their fortresses; and the Galata Tower, which dominates the Istanbul port, was part of the Genoese fortifications). A four-cornered fight then developed: Byzantines, Venetians, Genoese and Turks.

The Seljuk Turks' great period ended in the early thirteenth century, with the Mongol invasion. The Mongols were Turks of a sort, and Genghis Khan was a conqueror-genius. No one could defeat that archer-cavalry, and the Mongols, intelligently using foreigners with special skills, had a learning capacity as regards military techniques that allowed them to besiege and destroy city after city. If you surrendered, they left you more or less alone, but if you resisted, that was that, and a badge of Mongol rule was a pyramid of skulls, an Ottoman version of which is preserved at Niš, in Serbia. Russia, Persia, Seljuk Turkey succumbed, and so, via Afghanistan, did even northern India, though the Mughal dynasty was not established until later.

The Mongols were eventually stopped in Syria and Germany and, that, for a fairly simple reason: there was not enough grass for the horses, upon which cavalry empires depended. After a generation or two, the more sophisticated natives ran their empire, the Mongol or Turkish element supplying an aristocracy. This even applied in Egypt, in somewhat altered circumstances: the Mamelukes, who ran the place, were descended from Turkish Caucasus mercenaries, and the word itself means 'slave'.

The Mongols had smashed Persia in the thirteenth century, and had gone on to crush the Seljuks in Anatolia as well. Their state fragmented into various emirates, great and small. In north-western Anatolia, on the Byzantine border, there was a small one, its capital at an undistinguished place called Söğüt. This, like everything else, is disputed. The date of foundation is said to be 1300, but much of what happened in the early period consists of legend. The founder of this nucleus of the Ottoman state was called Osman (*c.* 1258–1324), and his father, Ertuğrul, was alleged to have come from the east, but writing was not the rulers' stock in trade: they were nomads, and the early archaeology (graves, rubbish dumps) is unrevealing.

There is a twentieth-century claim that the early Ottomans (which is a westernization of Osmanlı) were bright-eyed fighters for the cause of Allah, itself the answer to a rather Christian-triumphalist claim that they were noble savages who had had to learn everything from Byzantium, but the evidence either way is thin. An inscription on a mosque rooftop from the fourteenth century may or may not mean that the early Ottoman rulers saw themselves as Holy Warriors. But were they? They were certainly nomadic or semi-nomadic, many of them as such called Turcoman (recent migrants from Central Asia, not at home in towns) rather than Turkish; they spoke their own Turkish and not one of the grander languages. But Islam was a recent, thin growth; the pious complained at their habits; Osman's three main associates were Christians; his son Orhan (r. 1324–62) married a Byzantine princess; the court spoke Greek even a century later; there was no polygamy.

There is a rival theory that Osman was a classic frontiersman, waging a Wild West war on a richer neighbour, in which there is obvious truth. The Ottomans were fighters of genius, but they had to take statcraft from somewhere else. As an excellent Greek historian of all this, Stefanos Vryonis, says, you can play a good game by comparing the late Byzantine ways with those of the early Ottomans – land-measurement, taxes, laws, and even the type of contract that gave a knight land in exchange for fighting. It was only much later that the Holy Warrior idea came into vogue, and the school textbooks still put it about.

In 1326 Orhan captured the important town of Bursa, after an allegedly heroic siege. But the event did not really amount to much. The Byzantine governor gave up, complaining that his own state was collapsing, and converted to Islam. Most of the inhabitants, overtaxed, agreed. Many were Armenians, whose own form of Christianity was put down by the Orthodox Byzantines, and who had often been enthusiastic associates of the Turks from some way back. Their reward, come the Turkish conquest, was to have their religious headquarters moved into Constantinople, and for a long time they were known as *millet-i sadıka*, in effect 'the loyal nation'.

The fourteenth century, which saw the rise of the Ottoman state, is, as a chronicle, almost impossible to disentangle. The Black Death caused its mayhem. The actors on the stage were many, operating with changing alliances – there were Catalans in Greece, Hungarians in Bulgaria, Venetians and Genoese fighting each other over the Black Sea, while Byzantium endured a surreal twenty-years' civil war in which a blinded grandfather called John V briefly succeeded John VI (as Edward Gibbon remarks, 'the Greeks of Constantinople were animated only by the spirit of religion, and that spirit was productive only of animosity and discord'). Then there were the Ottoman Turks, who had a degree of military organization that made them valuable allies. Orhan slipped and slid between the factions, and in 1352, Genoese ships brought the Turks over the sea, for the first time, into Europe – the Balkans – to help one of them.

With Italian assistance, Orhan took over a rival emirate in north-western Anatolia, an episode left unmentioned by Muslim chroniclers, no doubt out of embarrassment at the Holy Warriors' somehow having missed their mission. They missed it in the other direction as well, taking Ankara from another of those emirates: the Alaeddin Mosque there commemorates this, and an inscription on it calls Orhan 'Sultan', a grand (and originally Arabic) title meaning 'lord of all'; it is the first time the term is used by the Turks. But when Orhan died, in 1362, the essential thrust was into the Balkans, and quite soon the Turks took the important old town of Adrianople (modern Edirne), making it their capital. His son, Murat I (r. 1362–89), went on (in the course of another Byzantine civil war) to take the great port city of Salonica, and much of northern Greece disintegrated. So did Bulgaria. In 1389, Lazar of Serbia met the Turks in a famous battle, that of Kosovo, and the Serbs, too, went under, though, out of vengefulness, one of their number managed to get close to Murat and assassinate him. Thereafter, the Serbs were closely associated with the Ottomans.

Murat was succeeded by his son Bayezit (r. 1389–1402), a very able man known as 'The Thunderbolt' (whose wife was a Serbian princess) and he rounded off the new Balkan possessions at Venice's expense. But his main contribution lay in Anatolia. There were other emirates, originally much grander than Osman's, and Bayezit took them over; then he moved east, essentially to control an important and lucrative trade route that ran to the port of Antalya from the Black Sea, which was in the possession of the powerful emirate of Karaman. Again, the point to be made is that he succeeded, as had his predecessors, because of his Balkan base, both the Serbs and the Byzantines marching with him. They could easily be enlisted to fight for the Ottomans, even if at other times they appealed to the West for help against them. The Byzantine emperor Manuel II Paleologus (r. 1391–1425) wrote a lament as he passed through the Black Sea area of Kastamonu. The name was a Turkish corruption of 'Castra Comneni', the camp of a once-leading Byzantine dynasty, and Manuel noted that 'the Romans had a name for the small plain where we now are, there are many cities here, but they lack the real splendour of a city, people. Most now lie in ruins.' True enough: the Turks were still nomadic.

The common people on the whole welcomed Turkish rule, which was honest and predictable: its taxes were lower, whereas the Latin administrations produced exactions and serfdom. There is, or was, even a theory to the effect that the somewhat heretical Christianity of those parts, and especially Bosnia, came from the Arian heresy, which denied that Christ was the Son of God and insisted only that He was a great prophet, much the same claim as is made in the Koran. The sources for this are not many or decisive. There was much Balkan conversion and extensive collaboration.

The Christian powers were alarmed at the Turks' advance. The Crusaders had been evicted from their mainland possessions in the Holy Land by a Muslim counteroffensive in 1291, but they still controlled the sea, and they took refuge in well-fortified islands, whether Rhodes or Cyprus (the ruler of which still called himself 'King of Jerusalem', passing the title on, eventually, to the Courteney family in Devon where, curiously enough, one of the last Paleologi was buried in the seventeenth century). The real problem for the Ottomans was Venice, dominating the trade of the eastern Mediterranean: rich, well run, unscrupulous, powerful. Resistance to the Turks was organized, if that is the correct word. The despairing Manuel II Paleologus made the rounds of the West, looking for support (and got it in words: he had even gone to London).

There was one powerful state to be brought in, Hungary. Oddly enough, the Hungarians, originally from Central Asia, were cousins of the Turks, the languages being built up on parallel lines, with many words in common ('barley', *arpa*, 'swim', *yüzmek* and *uszik*; 'saddle', *eyer* and *nyereg*; an oddity is 'tent': *çadır* and *sátor*, pronounced 'shator') and the Byzantines even referred to the Hungarian king (to whom they presented the crooked-cross crown) as *Tourkias archon*, 'prince of the Turks'. Later on, Hungarians had quite a role in Turkey, from an İbrahim Müteferrika who ran the first printing press in 1729 to Licco Amar, who organized violin teaching in the republic, and even to Atatürk's gardener.

The list takes in one Arminius Vámbéry, in the nineteenth century, who was the Isaiah Berlin of Istanbul. He was born Hermann Bamberger of a Jewish family that had been wiped out by an epidemic, was adopted by the local gentry family, changed his name to Vámbéry, became a Hungarian nationalist in the revolt against the Austrians in 1848, eventually made his way to Constantinople, learnt the language fast, was given confidential missions to Persia, and, once there, realized he must be quite close to the region from which the Hungarians had come. He went across deserts to enquire further. This led to the discovery, under the sands of the Taklamakan Desert, of an extraordinary civilization: Chinese, Indian and Hellenistic. The discoverer ended up weekending at Windsor Castle with Queen Victoria and was made a Commander of the Royal Victorian Order in 1902.

However, in 1396 Hungary was the bastion of Christianity. A European army attacked Bayezit in Bulgaria, and famously lost, in absurd circumstances, the battle of Nikopol. Here was a sign of things to come. The Turks had a modern army, whereas the Christians were still fighting pre-gunpowder wars, in which heavy cavalry, imprisoned in armour, charged off pretentiously after quarrelling leaders had windbagged away as to who would lead. Byzantium was for the moment saved because of an invasion from the east – one of the great recurring themes of Turkish history. The Turks themselves had come from the east, and so had the Mongols. Now, there appeared the last and most terrible of these invaders, Tamerlane.

He himself was a Turk of the Çagatay branch, like Genghis Khan, and in twenty-four years he reconstituted Genghis's vast empire with orgies of destruction. Pillars of skulls went up, including in the lands of the Golden Horde in Russia; when this monster died, in 1405, he had assembled a vast army for the conquest of China. Before then, he had wrecked Bayezit's growing Anatolian empire. There was a great battle at Ankara (on the site of the present airport) in 1402, in which Bayezit himself was captured.

The Anatolian emirs whom Bayezit had dispossessed had taken refuge with Tamerlane, and their men, conscripted by the Ottomans, deserted. Tamerlane had concealed war elephants in the forests which, back then, distinguished the Anatolian plateau (they do not distinguish it now) and the Ottoman forces disintegrated. So did Bayezit's state, as the emirs were restored. Byzantium had been saved, and was even able to take back Salonica because one of Bayezit's sons needed the emperor's help against a rival brother.

This ten-year period, the interregnum or *fetret*, has controversy attached to it, for much the same reason as does the foundation of the Ottoman state – did it work because it was Islamic or because it was crypto-European? Brother Süleyman co-operated with Byzantium, Venice and the Knights of St John, who represented the last vestige of the Crusades: the world, in other words, of the emerging Renaissance and, if you like, of rising capitalism. Might that not have been Turkey's future? But the story of Turkey is the victory of Anatolia, and then its being thrown away. It was the other brother, over the water in Anatolia, who won: Byzantium, as an ally, was now a dead weight. Mehmet I (r. 1413–21) reconstituted his father's empire, and his son, Murat II (r. 1421–51), now launched the Ottoman machine as the most formidable instrument of war in Europe.

Why did the Ottomans develop this formidable fighting machine? One answer is of course that that was the whole point. It was a military empire. It did not have an aristocracy: you rose if the Sultan promoted you, and you could obtain land if you promised to supply horsemen, but that did not mean that your family inherited it. On the non-military side, it was much the same, because a talented bureaucrat could build up rank and fortune, but might then, upon death (or execution, if the Sultan were in the mood) lose the lot. Early on there was something of an oligarchy, the Ottomans being the chiefs, but only just, and a great family such as the Candarlıs, powerful enough to be grand viziers and to have their own mosque – larger than any Ottoman mosque – in the old capital, Bursa (and, it seems, to have had their own trading relationship across the Bosphorus to Byzantium), could well count as equals. There were also Byzantine aristocrats who had converted and built up families of duration, such as Evrenos Bey, who conquered Greece for the Ottomans.

Contemporary writers were enraged when Mehmet II (r. 1451–81) broke with the rules of relative equality, and treated fellow emirs as subalterns, reducing them to submission because he had trained up an army of his own, from childhood. Again, when you look into this further, there is a Christian element – almost as if the Ottomans had set up a Byzantium that worked (and after all, three-quarters of their subjects were Christian). An essential component of the administration had made its appearance under Murat I: the Janissaries. In the later fourteenth century, as the Turks took over most of Greece, they hit upon the bright idea of conscripting young boys, giving them an education, making them convert to Islam and learn Turkish. Murat II developed this system (called *devşirme* or 'lifting'): the boys were awarded privileges at the palace and taught what they needed to know. Some boys graduated as pages to the Sultan and rose to run the state; others formed the nucleus of the new army, with a spirit of solidarity that other armies did not know. They were called 'new troops', *Yeni çeri* (which became Janissary in English), and they were a formidable force, with a strength and courage that enemies greatly feared and often admired. These Janissaries had their own music, their own distinctive style of ceremonial marching (two steps forward, one back, head to the side), and they had a formidable *esprit de corps*, with their own training grounds and barracks, or schools.

The Ottoman Sultans of the time were, of course, good leaders, glad to go off on campaign, and the courts at Edirne had a free-and-easy air to them, as people from anywhere and everywhere went in and out, the Sultans talking Greek or Turkish or Serbian. And there was another new element, the bombard. The Theodosian walls of Constantinople were not going to be able to resist.

By the mid-fifteenth century Byzantium had shrunk to the point that it consisted of just Constantinople and its hinterland; it was no more than a nuisance. The main interest now lay in Constantinople's dominating position on the trade route between the Black Sea and the Mediterranean, in which Venice and Genoa were rivals, and the Ottomans needed the money. The last real emperor, John VIII (r. 1425–48), appealed constantly to the West for help, and he travelled to Italy to ask in person. No one promised him anything much. The Pope had said he would do what he could, but only if the Byzantines accepted that he was the leader of the Church; they would have to give up their own Orthodoxy. The Byzantine powers-that-be might have been willing to do this but not the ordinary people, who hated the Latins in much the same way as the Russians shown in Sergei Eisenstein's film *Alexander Nevsky* (1938) hate the cruel and predatory Teutonic Knights. Nor were the clergy willing, as they could see that Russia would simply defect and take the leadership of Orthodoxy. John's successor, Constantine XI (r. 1449–53), decided to be bold. He provoked the Turks, refusing to pay the annual tribute expected of him, in the hope that the West would come to his assistance.

Murat II had initially retired and then died, and his young son, Mehmet II, was determined to put an end to the Constantinople anomaly. At the turn of 1452–53 he mustered a large army and a fleet. There was already, on the Asiatic side of the Bosphorus, a great castle, and Mehmet constructed another one on the European side, Rumeli Hisarı, much of it still in well-restored existence, at a narrow point where his guns could sink anything that tried to get by, thus blocking access to the city from the Black Sea. The walls of Constantinople had in the past been an insuperable obstacle to besiegers, of whom, over the centuries, there had been many. They had been built up since Roman times and were in places treble, very thick and well sited, in the sense that defenders could be concealed or would be able to make a sudden sally. An enemy fleet could not break into the Golden Horn because a huge chain, with floats, got in the way: its other end was fixed at Galata, which, in the hands of the Genoese, was neutral. Then there was the defensive speciality, Greek fire. However, by 1453, these arrangements for resisting attack had been overtaken.

Gunpowder had arrived from China in the fourteenth century, but guns were very difficult to cast, because, as you poured the iron, it might settle with tiny cracks that could prove fatal once the gun was used and the cracks, in the heat of the explosion, expanded. James II of Scotland was killed in 1460 when his big gun exploded and another great weapon – the Tsar Cannon (1586), now on display in the Kremlin – was never used, for example. Somehow, the Turks managed to make a workable monster. One Urban, the usual Hungarian, approached Constantine, offering his wares, but Constantine did not have any money; Mehmet II did. Urban created two monsters which, over a three-month period, were dragged by a team of sixty horses and three hundred men from Edirne to a spot at the walls that was vulnerable: a riverbed ran alongside and the walls had to be shaped accordingly, which made for weaker construction and blind spots. It was characteristic of Mehmet II that he followed the construction of these monsters very closely, understanding the techniques used by Urban to prevent the development of tiny fissures in the metal. They were then capable of firing a cannonball of vast weight: 450 kg or 1,000 lb (at this time, the French did not manage to fashion a cannonball of more than modest weight – 113 kg or 250 lb – and it could only bounce off walls). However, these were only the two largest: the Turks had a good hundred lesser guns.

The great walls could survive for a time, and the defenders were agile in repairing breaches, but there was a further problem: there were far too few troops to resist the attackers and Mehmet II had a very large army – 200,000 soldiers, many of them Christian. The walls were manned by 9,000 (some of them Muslim, adherents of one Orhan, a pretender to the Ottoman throne). Constantinople itself had shrunk in population to 50,000 people, and large areas of the city were deserted or in ruins (monks were selling off the historic marble of their monasteries to survive). Some of the ancient buildings had fallen down, and Constantine XI himself lived in the Palace of Blachernae, a smaller complex than the one-time Great Palace, which was in bad shape and too expensive to restore. The Genoese, who did, at Galata, have stout defences, remained neutral; they were not anxious to upset their arrangements for the profitable Turkish trade; in return, Mehmet II did not insist on their releasing their end of the chain. Instead, using rollers, he moved his ships bodily from the Bosphorus, at Beşiktaş (then called Diplokonion), to Kasımpaşa on the Golden Horn. There, they neutralized the Byzantine fleet, which otherwise might have done some damage. The Turks were now able to threaten another side of the walls, and thereby to thin out the defenders yet more. A breach of the walls where the guns had been concentrated completed the event: on 29 May 1453 the city was taken, Constantine XI being killed in the mêlée. The fall of Constantinople was a remarkable achievement for a state that had nearly collapsed fifty years before, and it sent shock waves across Europe.

TWO World Empire

Mehmet the Conqueror was only twenty-one when, on his white charger, he rode into captured Constantinople, and he had the same qualities as the young Napoleon – instant concentration, excellent judgment as regards subordinates, and a capacity to inspire them. He was, of course, a great military commander but, like Napoleon, he could also apply himself to the grind of state-building, including law. One of the Conqueror's first acts was to knock down the gigantic statue of Emperor Justinian that had dominated the square in front of the Hagia Sophia, but in effect he was set upon retaking the eastern Roman Empire that Justinian had made great in the sixth century. The money for the whole structure came largely from a poll tax levied on the Christians, who were then exempted from military service, and Mehmet II was very careful indeed not to alienate them: this was, after all, an empire in majority Christian, and in some ways it was even just Byzantium brought back to life. It was all something of a dramatic anticlimax.

The Orthodox Church collaborated with the new ruler. When the siege had started, there was a solemn ecumenical service with the Latin Christians in the Hagia Sophia. But the Orthodox hated it, their Grand Logothete (chancellor) famously saying that he preferred the Sultan's turban to the Cardinal's hat. The great church had been kept closed for the duration of the siege in case Orthodox and Catholics came to blows, and its doors were opened only at the very last moment. Mehmet called in a prominent Orthodox dissident, the scholar-monk, Gennadios. They talked in Greek, and a document was drawn up giving Gennadios the title 'Patriarch', the rank and badges of an Ottoman general, and rights of property that made him the largest landowner in the empire. He was addressed, as was the custom for Byzantine rulers, as *megas authentes*, 'great prince'. (At this time the Turks, not unlike their (very) remote cousins the Japanese, had great difficulty in pronouncing certain letters or combinations of them. A main town in Cappadocia, Prokopi, was turned into Ürgüp, Sandraka became Zonguldak, and Palaeokastron became Balıkesir. *Authentes*, as the Turkish tongue pronounced it, became *efendi,* an honorific throughout the Middle East to this day.) Co-operation between the new ruler and the Christians was such that if the Sultan wanted music he snapped his fingers and sent for the Orthodox choir. True, Hagia Sophia was converted into a mosque, but the Orthodox kept nearly all of the other churches.

The majority of the Byzantines stayed on, and prospered: Constantine's nephews rose high, one of them to be viceroy of Rumelia, as the Ottomans called their possessions in the southern Balkans. Byzantine aristocrats who had converted to Islam also built mosques – Has Murat Paşa in Aksaray, on the western side of the city, by the walls, and Rum Mehmet Paşa in Üsküdar, the old Scutari, on the Asian side of the Bosphorus. Both of them are recognizably Byzantine in construction, with thin, flat bricks ingeniously put together to withstand earthquakes. In the early sixteenth century, there was a Cantacuzene (though he called himself Spandugnino) of Byzantine aristocratic origin who wrote a book describing the close blood relations still existing between leading Venetians and prominent Turks.

Konstantiniye, as the Ottomans called their new capital (the later 'Istanbul' was, in this writer's opinion, just a Turkish corruption, like Ürgüp), needed to be rebuilt: the Conqueror, fully aware that he was succeeding Rome, applied himself. The present-day Grand Bazaar was put up in the old centre, together with assorted *hans*, hygienically designed places where merchants could stable their pack animals and store their goods safely. Constantinople doubled in population and by 1580 was a city of 750,000 people, far larger than any other European city, and western

European paintings and engravings of its setting and major features reveal much admiration.

To some Muslim grumbling, Mehmet allowed the Greeks to return. He moved in Jews and Armenians as well, neither of whom had been welcome under Byzantium. In the Genoese quarter of Galata, over the Golden Horn, foreigners ('Franks' – the Turkish word for syphilis is *frengi*) were also permitted to reside, without molestation, and, as trade grew with the return of stability, the Venetians especially became important. Guilds, themselves tightly supervised, controlled prices and maintained very high standards for quality.

Mehmet ignored the palaces of the Byzantine emperors and put up structures of his own – yet another great castle, the Seven Towers, by the main ceremonial entrance to the city, the Golden Gate, while work went speedily ahead on a new palace, the site, now, of Istanbul University. It was built rather on Byzantine lines, and Mehmet got bored with it. He also constructed his own mosque (Fatih Mosque), with all the usual additions of hospitals and schools, on the site of the knocked-down church where the early Byzantine emperors had been buried. Work then started on the palace that was to become the brain centre of the entire empire, what is now known as the Topkapı (meaning 'Cannon Gate', from its situation on the old walls). It has the finest setting of any palace in the world, on a small peninsula overlooking the Golden Horn at the junction of the Bosphorus and the Sea of Marmara, and it was built on a very human scale, with great gardens stretching down to the water's edge.

Here, behind thick and high walls, Mehmet II made a mystery of himself, protected from the public gaze by a Janissary guard utterly foreign to the locals, wearing elaborate uniforms and making their own clashing music. His predecessors had generally been much more approachable. Now, a huge imperial court was taking shape, eventually to employ 30,000 people – sixty of them just to make the cakes, for instance, and dozens of others appointed to the Sultan's personal service as keeper of the linen or holder of the stirrup (*rikabdar*). There was a corps of food-tasters, headed by the chief taster (*çaşnıgirbaşı*), and there were pages detailed to stay with the Sultan as he slept, partly because of the danger of a nocturnal assassination. The officials involved were entirely dependent upon him, as they had no life outside: they had started out as Christian boys, taken from their homes by the *devşirme*. They were converted to Islam and sent to stay with a Turkish family before undergoing the rigours of the court-page school; the best of them were taken into court service, and they could rise to the very top of Ottoman society, as grand viziers or provincial governors. There was, later on, much denunciation of this system, but it affected only a miniscule proportion of the Balkan population, and in any case was less cruel than the equivalent in, say, Henry VI's England, when Eton was established as a public school to train scholarship boys for the royal service. In fact, Muslim families sometimes paid their Christian neighbours to pass off a son of theirs as the Christians' own.

In comparison with what was to come, Mehmet II was quite modest, but the world-empire system goes back to him. By odd coincidence, he even contrived to die, in 1481, at much the same place as Constantine had done (it is called Gebze, about thirty miles east of Istanbul on the Asian side of the Sea of Marmara, and Hannibal had also committed suicide there; it is now an industrial landscape that provokes in the passer-by some sympathy). When Mehmet died, the Pope staged a three-day ceremony of thanksgiving, bells clanging, cardinals processing. It was not well timed, for the Sultan's victories were only the start: within two generations, this empire would be everywhere, reaching out to the Atlantic coast of Morocco, the gates of Vienna, the heart of Persia, and even as far as Indonesia.

Mehmet II could not anticipate this, and in the later fifteenth century, both he and his son still faced formidable opposition. There was, in the north, Hungary, quite capable of intervening in the southern Balkans, and in the west there was powerful, shrewdly managed opposition from Venice as well. She still ran much of Greece, and owned islands in the Aegean, from which her galleys could strike at Ottoman shipping; and on the eastern coast of the Adriatic, Dalmatia, there was a string of port towns, built on Venetian lines, which allowed her to interfere inland. In mountainous Albania, there was a long war between the Turks and the local hero, Scanderbeg. These wars, though religious in paraphernalia and also in justification, were really about natural resources, and trade.

On the Bosnian–Serbian border, there were silver mines – Srebrenica, the town which saw massacres in the Yugoslav wars in the 1990s, owes its name to the Slavonic word for 'silver' – and Mehmet badly needed the metal to support a currency that would otherwise have descended into copper scrap: conquests paid for themselves. The battles with Venice extended into the Black Sea, because this was the high road for the Russian trade in furs and, for that matter, slaves: the present-day Turkish word for 'prostitute', *orospu*, is medieval Persian, and the central part of it denotes 'Rus'. The Genoese bases in and around the Crimea were valuable property; so too was the deep-water port of Trebizond (modern Trabzon), on the southern coast of the Black Sea, still an 'empire' in the hands of the Byzantine Comnenos dynasty.

On the north-western side of the Black Sea, there were also trade routes and natural resources of some importance, in lands historically called 'the Danubian principalities', and their rulers, sometimes in concert with the Hungarians, made trouble. The famous one, Vlad the Impaler (1431–76), is the original of 'Dracula', known for fantastic cruelty: impalement – a very sharp, thin, stave being inserted into the rectum, and then pushed carefully and very slowly upwards, avoiding any of the vital organs, to emerge in the victim's neck. If the impaler got it wrong, such that the victim died quickly, he was himself impaled, and the ruler of Wallachia carried out this punishment in thousands of cases at once.

The Turks won, but it took time, and both Mehmet II and his son Bayezit II (r. 1481–1512) had much clearing-up to do. Their armies, dragging artillery through mire, and in the case of Trebizond, up and around (and sometimes down off) the high mountain tracks of the Pontus, took time. However, by the time Mehmet died, these areas were taken over: Serbia in 1459, Athens and the Morea by 1460 (the King of Spain is still in title

'Duke of Athens'), Bosnia in 1463, Wallachia, southern of 'the Danubian principalities', in 1476, Albania in 1478, Herzegovina in 1482. In the Black Sea, Mehmet's best general, Gedik Ahmet Pasha, had to fight a difficult amphibious action, together with complicated Tatar allies, in order to conquer the Italian trading ports of the Crimea and the Sea of Azov, but when Bayezit took over, the Black Sea had become an Ottoman lake, more or less closed to western shipping. Its trade helped fill the treasury, which, given the weight of military expenditure, needed filling.

Expansion was to resume, and on an enormous scale, but when Mehmet II died, there was a lull, which showed one, and perhaps the main, weakness of the emerging imperial system. If the old Sultan died, who was to succeed him? The early Ottomans had followed Roman guidelines, eldest son following father, and the sons had generally been given some sort of apprenticeship in government. However, there was nothing much to prevent an ambitious younger brother from collecting malcontents and launching a challenge for the succession, and, here, the interregnum that had followed upon the death of Bayezit I in the first years of the century was a warning, because the state itself had nearly disintegrated. Besides, there was, legitimized by the traditions of Central Asia, a more practical form of succession: let the most experienced male member of the ruling house take over – generally a brother, sometimes a cousin. This was how Genghis Khan had managed matters, as no tribe would wish to be run by an inexperienced boy, with some regent or other who might murderously cultivate his own garden. Mehmet himself had given this matter some thought, and, since he spent much of the time on thick codes of law, sanctioned the practice of fratricide: when you succeed to the throne, murder your brothers. He did this himself in one case, and Bayezit now faced the same problem.

The trick in these circumstances was for the men in the know to conceal for as long as possible the fact of the old Sultan's death, so that the successor whom they favoured could make his move first. Bayezit was their favoured candidate, and took up the reins in Constantinople, paying the Janissaries to be on his side. His brother Cem, with a local power base in Anatolia, and allies among various dissident elements, raised the standard of revolt, marched on Constantinople, and lost. Bayezit drove into Anatolia. Cem managed to escape, and spent almost twenty years as a gilded prisoner in Muslim Egypt or in Christian Europe, a focus – and possible standard bearer – for any ruler worried at the expansion of the Ottoman Empire.

It is a sad and rather revealing story. Cem took refuge with the Knights of St John on the island of Rhodes, just off the Anatolian coast. The Knights of St John – they still exist, and are involved with medical charities – had been warrior monks at the time of the great Crusades, and, when these ended, had set up castles with extraordinarily thick walls (that of today's Bodrum, on a peninsula, was constructed from the ruins of one of the Seven Wonders of the World, the Mausoleum of Halicarnassus). Their chief place was on Rhodes, which was large enough to sustain a substantial fleet of galleys, and these galleys operated piratically, much to the profit of the Knights. In 1480 Mehmet II had tried and failed to root them out. They made a great fuss of Cem, making sure just the same that he did not go far.

In 1482, Bayezit himself was abashed enough to offer the Knights a large annual sum for his brother to be kept in good state; the negotiations (conducted in Greek, one of the Turks' negotiators being a Byzantine nobleman) were managed in a dignified and indeed friendly style, but it was blackmail just the same. Cem and his brother even exchanged poems and gifts. In the event, the Knights carried him off to France (the journey from Rhodes to Nice took forty-five days, even in calm seas) and then from pillar to post until the Pope purchased him. He eventually died of disease, and maybe exile-despair, in Naples; whereupon Bayezit bought the body, preserved in a lead coffin, and had it ceremonially buried in the great tomb complex of the Ottoman dynasty, the Muradiye, at Bursa, the first real capital. Then he murdered Cem's surviving descendants (one of them got away with the Knights, when Rhodes at last fell to the Ottomans in 1522. He converted to Christianity, acquired a title from the Pope, and has a chief descendant in Australia).

With this weapon in his hands, Pope Innocent VIII, elected in 1484, wanted to organize a new crusade before the Ottomans took over any more of Christian Europe, and from Rome the old appeals went out for a new Holy League, to support Hungary and Venice. The Pope, at that time, was himself something of a military asset, as his lands in Italy contained mines of alum, then an extremely valuable mineral, a sort of salt that had medicinal uses and was especially useful in producing an essential dye mordant for wool. The money from this, and of course from the famous indulgences by which contributors to papal coffers were offered a reduction to their term in Purgatory, supported a small war fleet and bought Swiss mercenaries. There were, however, problems. Pope Innocent was not the ideal figure to be launching Holy War, given that he had two illegitimate children, and was engaged in a lengthy intrigue to marry one of them to the daughter of Lorenzo de' Medici of Florence, who agreed, on condition that his thirteen-year-old son was made a cardinal.

However, the call to Holy War disunited Christian Europe. The Venetians, with the trade of the eastern Mediterranean to think of, egged everyone else on, but secretly told Bayezit what was happening. No one trusted the Hungarians, who wasted much of their wealth on showing off, with an embassy to France consisting of scores of people all dressed in the same outfits and bringing elaborate presents. Fanatical Spaniards were enthusiastic, but had their hands full in North Africa. Each ruler, as in the days of the Cold War, was fighting his own version of the Holy War, and in the case of France was often not fighting it at all. The Pope did stage a great conference in Rome in 1490, and, again as in Cold War days, it attracted all manner of bores, adventurers and braggarts – poor Cem, some stray Byzantine pretenders, a fake Georgian prince or two, men wanting money to print unreadable tracts, Portuguese waffling at length, Hungarians going on about their woes, the English trying to be sensible. Eventually, a Holy League was indeed formed, but it then attacked Venice in 1508, spearheaded by the Pope, who quite speedily turned around, took up alliance with Venice, and attacked the others. The would-be crusade sank with all hands.

What saved the situation for the Europeans in the medium term was another of the great perennial problems of the Turks, one that in the end destroyed their empire: the east. If Holy War on the Christian side had its problems, on the Muslim side these were, if anything, worse. In 1500, the greatest city in the eastern Mediterranean was still Cairo, and Egypt, under its Mameluke rulers, was a great naval power. She was also rich, as so much trade (spices, sugar, coffee) came in from the Indian Ocean through the Red Sea, and because pilgrims, paying substantial sums for protection, had to make their way to Mecca and Medina as part of their religious obligations. Someone had said, as the Crusades ebbed away, that you could control Palestine only from Egypt, and the rulers of Egypt did indeed rule there, and not just Syria but south-eastern Anatolia as well. In the time of Bayezit II they were still established in central Anatolia: he had to fight difficult wars with them, and his forces did not prosper, while they took an interest in Cem as pretender to the Ottoman throne, and all along the Knights of St John played both sides.

But there were further difficulties for the Turks. At least wars with Egypt did not concern the very nature of the state and religion. This happened with the Ottoman relationship with Persia, which raised itself again and again. This was to preoccupy Sultans just as much as did Central Europe, at any rate until the later eighteenth century, when the comparative weakness of both Ottomans and Persians *vis-à-vis* Russia made their historic rivalry look picturesque and archaic. Persia's was of course a great civilization, once capable of challenging the Roman Empire itself. However, somehow it had gone wrong: it had fallen to the Arabs, adopted their Islam, recovered, and had then been taken over by the Great Seljuks, superior cousins of the Seljuks who were taking over Anatolia. Both were then swamped by Mongols, and then Persia was struck by Tamerlane, with vast destructive energy, around 1400. The Anatolian rulers survived much better, being more remote and poorer, and this was one of the reasons for the emergence of the Ottomans themselves. True, they had been defeated by Tamerlane, but very soon he just went away, and the Ottoman forward march was resumed, in this case towards the east, and of course the lands of Persia, which at that period included Azerbaijan and Baghdad. In Mehmet the Conqueror's time, this had meant a war, in the end successful, to take over some of the lands belonging to the Black Sheep tribal federation, roughly based in south-eastern Anatolia. It had absorbed much of the territory (to north and north-east) of a rival federation, the White Sheep, and had then spread out over a Persia already desperately weakened under Tamerlane, in a huge but superficial empire, as far as Afghanistan.

However, a new Persia was emerging under all of this. When the White Sheep had lost, a remnant kept going in remote and mountainous regions to the east of the present-day north-eastern Turkish border. Here, in the later fifteenth century, are the origins of the Safavid dynasty, which in time, and for the next two centuries, represented an indestructible barrier to Ottoman eastward expansion. The Safavids began around 1500 with a religious challenge: their founder, Shah Ismail, advertised a sort of anti-Ottoman religious ideology. The details of this have to do with the right to the Prophet's succession and mean little to the outsider. It is called Shiism, from an Arabic word meaning 'follower' (of Ali, the might-have-been successor, buried in Iraq). This came up, as an inspirational form of Islam, as distinct from the repetitive oppressiveness of the sometimes ultra rule-bound Sunni version, which had the Ottoman Sultan and his pashas, beys and muftis at its head. It was not just that the Ottomans were Sunni. They were also western and even European; Christian soldiers who had converted were taking over the land of stout Muslims.

The Safavids had a good start, as regards the territories of Azerbaijan proper, but Shiism also spread into eastern Anatolia, where there were nomadic tribesmen, wandering around in the ruins of the emirates that had been broken by Mehmet II. More than that: there always were, in central and western Anatolia, elements so disaffected from the rising power of the Ottoman Empire that they broke out into open revolt. In the mid-fourteenth century, as Orhan I and Murat I extended their power eastwards, they dealt harshly with guilds of artisans, the Ahi brotherhoods, especially strong in the Ankara region; and during the interregnum there was a full-scale revolt in western Anatolia, crushed with great difficulty by a sheikh whose followers were exiled to the east. To them, Shiism spoke.

However, there was no agreed corpus of Shiism, and much depended upon local traditions (some of them, in Turkey, obviously Christian). At any rate, a movement grew up in the later fifteenth century, in eastern Anatolia, and its adepts were known as 'redheads' – *Kızılbaş* – because they wore a tall red turban with twelve folds in it, indicating the number of caliphs whose authority they accepted. For them, the messiah (of which 'mahdi', in Turkish *mehdi*, is the translation) was immanent and imminent. They did not much respect the Ottomans, and were banned from Constantinople in 1502. However, their patron and inspiration Shah Ismail grew stronger: he claimed to be a sort of messiah, his followers not vulnerable to anything; he took Baghdad in 1508, and sent word to Venice that he would welcome an alliance. In 1510 he attacked Trebizond, which was governed by Bayezit's son Selim, who was, however, instructed by his father not to resist: the old man was tired and disillusioned, wanted only peace. There had been a great earthquake in Constantinople in 1509, and Bayezit took up residence in the old capital, Edirne. Selim, who had married a daughter of the Giray dynasty in the Crimea, and was a man of altogether different stamp, took refuge with his own son, Süleyman, who governed in the Crimea – not just a different man again, but set to be the greatest Sultan of them all.

Then in 1511 a province in south-western Anatolia itself erupted. On the great date of mourning in the Shia calendar, Aşure, which commemorates the murder of Hussein, in the Shia view the rightful successor to the Prophet, there was a *Kızılbaş* rising. It was led by a ranter with charisma who passed himself off as the Messiah, one Şahkulu, called Karabıyıklıoğlu ('son of

Black Whiskers') Hasan the Caliph. This was not just a peasants' revolt. It was joined by former soldiers who had lost their grace-and-favour lands to Christians who had fought well for the Sultan, and by nomadic tribesmen who resented the growing power of the state, with all its grandiose works. Selim's brother, the local governor, retreated to Antalya castle, on the southern coast, and the Şahkulu army wandered around, rampaging, burning mosques, and capturing another governor, who was impaled and slow-roasted. Then the rebels marched east, proclaiming allegiance to Shah Ismail; and the movement stopped only when Hasan was killed in a drawn battle near Sivas, where the Ottoman commander was also killed. It was obvious enough that Bayezit II had lost control, and his sons started fighting for the succession. Now, a sign of things to come, it was the Janissaries, the great elite regiments, that made the difference. They chose Selim in 1512, and he ordered his father into exile, whereupon the old man, maybe done away with, died. Then Selim disposed of a good dozen brothers and nephews who might have challenged him.

Selim acquired the name 'the Grim'. 'Tough' (*Yavuz*) is a better rendering, but there is a parallel in Russia, where 'the Terrible', for Ivan IV, a near-contemporary, is a similar distortion of *grozny*, 'threatening'. Ivan IV (who killed his own son in a drunken rage) was the maker of the all-powerful Tsarist autocracy in Russia, in effect cutting back the powers of the old nobility and the church, sometimes with tremendous cruelty, and generally by using Tatar helpers. Selim operated in much the same way. It was he who wrenched the empire from its hinges and, in a few years (he died in 1520), made it something else, enormous, and, to the Christian world, terrifying. As Macaulay remarked of Frederick the Great's father, Selim was a cross between Moloch and Puck. He tended to execute viziers, one of whom enquired if he could be given advance notice of his execution, so as to put his affairs in order, to which Selim said, yes, but would he wait until a replacement had been found. Again, like Frederick the Great's father, he was almost fanatically aware that the treasury needed to be filled, at whatever cost in meanness and exaction. This formidable figure now mustered his 80,000 men in 1514 and prepared to deal with Persia.

Ottoman society was, as they said of eighteenth-century Prussia, 'hatched from a cannonball' – in fact, this was almost literally true, because its military successes did come in large part from prowess in artillery. For a good century after Mehmet II's death in 1481, the Ottoman Empire seemed to be almost unbeatable, and after the fall of Constantinople it expanded and expanded. There were more and better guns; Turkish cavalry was also superior; and besides, these Sultans had a standing army, whereas everyone else had mercenaries or museum pieces. The Sultans took talent where they found it, and when the Jews of Spain were expelled in the early sixteenth century, they sought refuge in the Ottoman Empire, particularly in Salonica and Smyrna (modern İzmir), the great ports. The millions of non-Muslims, paying the special tax that also exempted them from military service, paid for a large part of the structure. It was a military empire, very strictly regulated, and the bureaucratic machinery whirred away registering the trade and land, producing the troops much more efficiently than did the empire's enemies. This needed determined direction, and, under Selim, got it.

The *Kızılbaş* were now concentrated in north-central Anatolia, where they were cheated into registering as such. Forty thousand of them were massacred, and they scattered into the hills, some of them, in the desolate and barely accessible Dersim region, to adopt the Zaza (a Persian word meaning 'stutter') form of Kurdish. In time, these *Kızılbaş* became what is known in modern Turkey as Alevis, to which subject we shall, much later, return. Then the army was marched, muttering mutiny, through difficult terrain and horrible heat to deal with Shah Ismail. He was setting up the Safavid state, but faced endless difficulties, especially with his own east, where the Uzbeks threatened him, and in any case his army was not up to Janissaries and Ottoman gunnery. Near Lake Van, at Çaldıran in August 1514, his horse archers were put to flight, and Selim had a new frontier, with, already, a foothold in the lands of today's Iraq.

The next step, even more fateful, was Egypt. The Mameluks had made endless trouble for Constantinople and with their fabled riches from trade they provided an obvious target for Selim, who trundled his gunnery and Janissaries to effect against them. The Mamelukes were still really only any good at cavalry charges: Selim took Aleppo, Damascus, and then Cairo itself (1517). This made him master of the Arab world, and Ottoman authority stretched across it, to North Africa, the 'Maghreb', a derivation of an Arabic word meaning 'west' (*garb*). It reached, as well, to the Holy Places of Mecca and Medina, and ultimately to the Yemen, which controlled the mouth of the Red Sea, and even to Ethiopia, which for a century was Turkish.

The Mamelukes had re-established the caliphate, once located at Baghdad, in Cairo, and their man claimed the Prophet's succession (the meaning of the word). Selim now took over the caliphate, along with its various trophies and symbols – hairs of the beard of the Prophet; his (or more probably Ali's) sword, *Zülfikar*; a footprint; and other relics now preserved in a special *köşk* of the Topkapı museum. The caliphate of all Islam was a grand title, but for a long time it did not mean very much in practice, or even anything at all. But the acquisition of Egypt, along with the taking of Baghdad, did wrench the centre of gravity of the empire away from the Christian Balkans towards the Arab world, and changed its character. By the time he died, Selim was in grandiose mode, and he took the titles, *Malik ul-Barreyn, wa Khakan ul-Bahrayn, wa Kasir ul-Jayshayn, wa Khadim ul-Haramayn* – meaning, *King of the Two Continents, Ruler of the Two Oceans, Conqueror of the Two Armies* (European and Persian)*, and Servant of the Two Holy Shrines* (Mecca and Medina). His son was to add, 'Marcher Lord of the Horizon', 'Rock that Bestrides the Continents', and 'Shadow of God on Earth'; his satellite, the ruler of the Crimea, addressed the Tsar in rescripts that started off, 'The immortal declaration of the Khan that concerns you is as follows ...' Megalomania beckoned, but for a time reality was not too far from it.

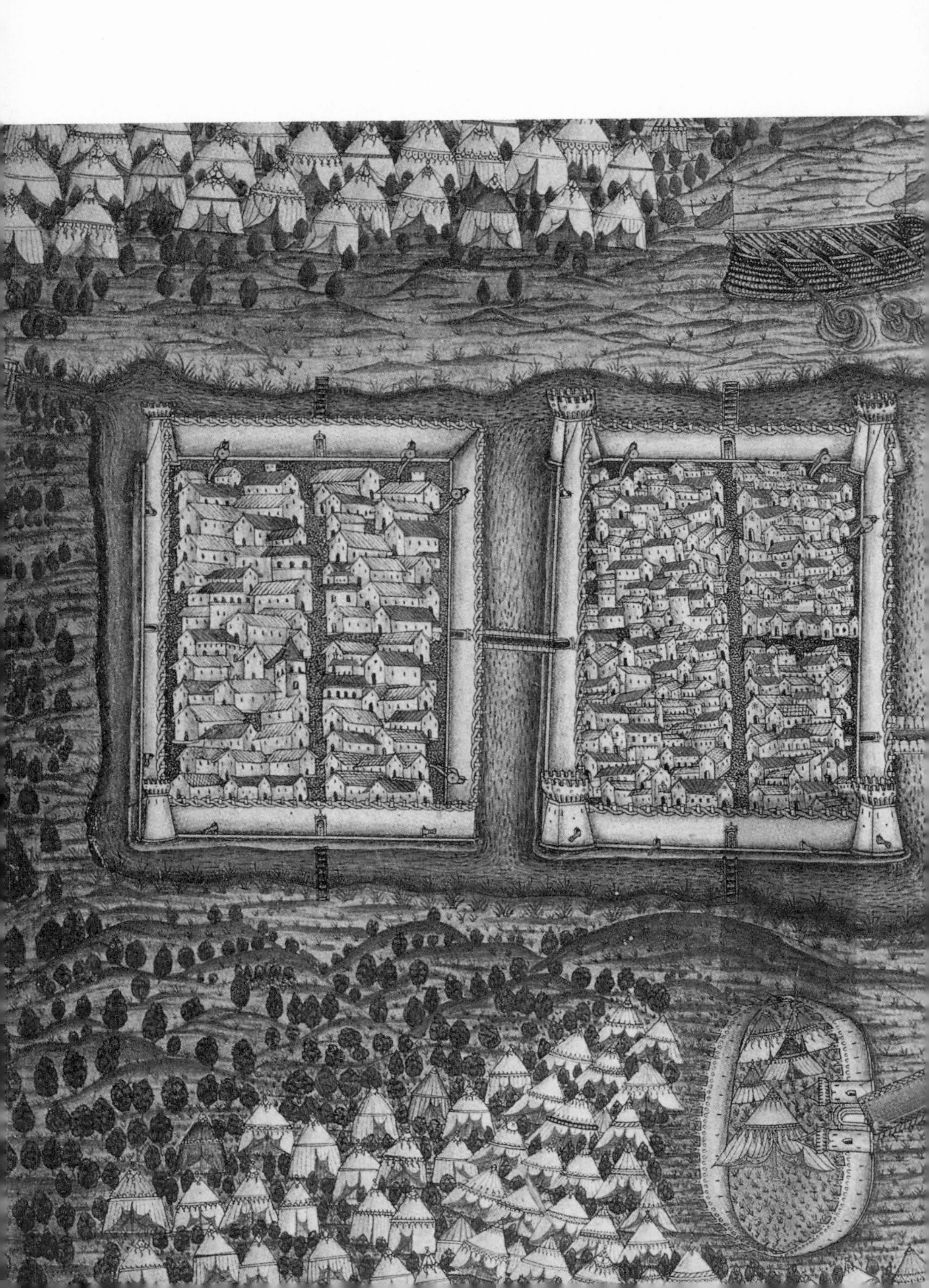

THREE Zenith

Selim's son, Süleyman I, took over smoothly, there being no fraternal wars to fight. He was to rule for almost fifty years (1520–66) and the reign was the high point of the Ottoman Empire. Its gunnery specialists were in Indonesia, its fleet wintering at Toulon, its armies fighting in Hungary, on the Volga and on the lower Tigris. Constantinople was an extraordinarily rich place, and, with nearly 750,000 inhabitants, was three times larger than Paris. It was a brilliant period, in jurisprudence as in poetry, and it is commemorated by the grandest of the city's mosques, particularly the Sülemaniye, the Sultan's own. Süleyman himself had his great-grandfather's gifts of instant concentration on each of a row of different problems, as with a sort of strategic three-dimensional chess. To the Turks he is *Kanunî*, the law-maker. To the Germans he was *der grosse Türck*, the Great Turk, and Titian paid homage to him with a superb portrait, now in Vienna. As with Napoleon, there were a dozen great campaigns, with armies of 200,000, and hundreds of guns, marshalled with extraordinary efficiency and drive. The Habsburg ambassador said that 'of the three continents which share our hemisphere, each contributes its share to our destruction. Like a lightning bolt, he strikes, shatters and destroys whatever is in his way.'

The year 1520 is a good date. The Reformation, printing, the spread of knowledge, map-making and a new astronomy were underway, whether, like the old East German ministry of culture, you want to call it all 'the early bourgeois revolution' or not. Then there are the beginnings of European empire building, and here, with Süleyman, there was to be a great clash, for megalomania was in vogue. The Habsburg dynasty had also started off from very modest beginnings in the thirteenth century, and had made its way up in a few generations, first to the German Empire, and then to the thrones of Spain. It also addressed itself to the public, incorporating acknowledgments to heaven, with a list of titles – fifty-one, in the Austrian case, including mysterious bits and pieces such as Pont-à-Mousson and the *gefürstete Grafschaft Görz*, but in the Spanish case, at least by implication, it had much more, given that Madrid ran Latin America and had been awarded that hemisphere by the Pope.

In 1492, Queen Isabella of Castile and her consort, King Ferdinand of Aragon, had cleared the last Muslim king from Granada, and in the same year had sent Colombus off on his voyage to America. Then Spain carried her war with the Muslims into North Africa, and the Ottomans also became involved there, from the other end of the Mediterranean. It was Christianity versus Islam, a battle between Charles V of Spain and his son Philip II on the one side, Süleyman I and his son Selim II on the other. You might even say that by 1600 they had fought each other to a ruinous standstill, because neither really recovered, though the process of degeneration was long drawn out. Building fleets of 300 galleys took huge amounts of wood, a process damaging to forests which, in any event, were increasingly badly maintained, as the sheer expense of wars and bases weakened the state's organization in other matters.

The comparison of Spain and Turkey is an interesting one. Spain had had seven centuries of Islamic rule, and the era of the caliphate at Cordova had at times out-rivalled even the very grand Cairo. El Cid, the eleventh-century hero of alleged liberation, had in fact an arabic name – a version of 'Said' meaning 'lord'. In the seventeenth century, Turkey and Spain fell behind the West in obvious ways, shown in military encounters. Each had a tangential and cantankerous relationship to Europe. A minority in Spain, the Catalans, adapted; so did Greeks and Armenians in Turkey. Other minorities, the Basques and the Kurds, often very aggressively, did not (in modern times ETA and the PKK have co-operated). In the nineteenth century, the army in both cases was entering politics, in the case of Spain, dramatically so, and you would not have much trouble in comparing the role of religion in both countries, either. Madrid and Ankara are both artificial capitals, without economic activity between penpushing and bootbashing: it is Barcelona that should be compared with Istanbul. However, both Madrid and Ankara are placed in a treeless plateau, with extremes of climate, and the trees disappeared, maybe because of climate change, around 1650, more probably because the landowning arrangements collapsed, such that peasant sheep and goats were allowed to damage the bark and the roots.

There is a strange parallel later on because of this – railways. In the nineteenth century, the Spanish tried to overcome their backwardness by constructing these, as did the Turks somewhat later. However, in the Iberian soil and climate, laying rails was difficult: the iron expanded in the summer and contracted in the winter, and the rails became bent. Trains went slowly, with frequent accidents, making a loss. The Spanish railways were so badly indebted that there was no money for modernization, and the state had to arrange for the manufacture of obsolete spare parts. It took twelve hours even in the 1960s to go from Madrid to Barcelona, roughly 300 miles. The Turkish case was not as dismal, but even now the night journey from Ankara to Istanbul, a comparable distance, takes over nine hours, although (sadly: it is the last old-fashioned sleeping car in Europe) this is set to change. The Spanish solved their problem only when motorway technology allowed proper communications, and the resulting money, at some remove, made possible the modernization of the railways. In the 1980s, Turkey underwent a similar experience, and, with some aptness, Spanish engineers and rolling stock are now involved in making Anatolian railways up to date. The Ankara–Istanbul journey will take three or four hours, as does the Madrid–Barcelona one.

As the sixteenth century got under way, the Spanish and Ottoman empires were gradually coming into conflict. The essential element was the

Ottoman control of Egypt. In the first place, the revenues covered two-thirds of the budget, because Cairo was such a nodal point, with connections as far as Indonesia and all over North Africa. Then again, there was the caliphate. The Mamelukes had not quite known what to do with it, were even embarrassed by the allies that it brought, but at the very least an Ottoman Sultan designated Successor of the Prophet could count on doors opening in North Africa. This happened. One after another, the chieftains of the long coastal strip, as far as Algeria in the west, accepted Janissary garrisons, swore loyalty, and sometimes meant it. The rulers of Morocco were a different matter, for theirs was a large and rich country with an Atlantic coast, and their dynasty looked down on Turks; it was often disinclined, in matters of religion, to see what the fuss was about, although for two decades Morocco accepted Ottoman suzerainty. In the same way, as we have seen, through Egypt, the Ottoman hand fell on much of Arabia, Yemen, and Ethiopia, on the other side of the Red Sea.

Even here, an Iberian issue was being opened up, though this time it concerned Portugal rather than Spain. In the middle of the fifteenth century the first notes of a considerable overture had been sounded, when Portuguese ships started to explore the Atlantic, the Azores, and then crept down along the West African coast, setting up trading posts. The creeping, with favourable currents, carried them to the Cape of Good Hope, and then into the Indian Ocean. In 1498 Vasco da Gama reached India, there to encounter discomfited Arab traders, who had some idea who he was and what he meant. Europe needed spices from the east, and up to this point the Arabs and Venice had had the monopoly, whether by sea to Suez or by camel-caravan to Aleppo. Now, the Portuguese could dramatically undercut their prices by taking the direct sea route, and they were soon involved in Indonesia, the main source. Once in Egypt, the Ottomans stood to lose, and the trade routes through the Red Sea or the Persian Gulf began to suffer; there were even fears that the Portuguese could affect the pilgrimage road to Mecca. The Portuguese viceroy of India, Albuquerque, seemed to be all-powerful, with ships that sailed better and had superior gunnery, although he never had more than 5,000 of his own countrymen to command. The Portuguese even invaded Bahrain, to block the trade through Basra, which the Ottomans had occupied. It was for this reason that the Ottomans took over Yemen and Ethiopia, to guard the entrance to the Red Sea, and there were battles with the Portuguese as far away as Zanzibar (which, as *Zenci bahr*, means sea of the black people in old Turkish). Süleyman sent guns to a ruler in Indonesia who complained that he was under threat; his advisers went to India. As early as 1513, an Ottoman cartographer, a former pirate named Piri Reis, made a map of the world, including South America, that is uncannily accurate. However, though sometimes presented as a first stage in world imperialism, these affairs were sideshows, as the chief battles were fought in the Mediterranean.

Under Mehmet II, Turkish expeditions had ravaged even Otranto, in southern Italy, and once the Turks had established themselves in the Maghreb, they could use the pirates of what was called 'the Barbary coast'. Some of these even managed to reach Rome, causing the Pope to flee. They managed this, in part, because 'Christendom' was not solid. The Reformation had broken out in Germany, and spread to the Netherlands; long religious wars resulted, and at the siege of Leiden in 1574, the Protestant defenders proclaimed 'lief turk den paus' – 'better Turk than Papist' in free translation. The French went one better. Though himself Catholic, Francis I was quite willing to take up a Turkish alliance if this did down his main enemy, the Habsburg ruler of Spain and the Netherlands, Charles V, who was the chief rival of Süleyman. Turkish ships were allowed to winter at Toulon, and the Christians' position in the Mediterranean suffered accordingly. The Knights of St John had already been expelled from Rhodes after a very long siege in 1522. Cyprus, then controlled by Venice, was also to be taken, in 1571 (that was Othello's battle) – an easy conquest to start with, because the Orthodox Greek population much preferred the Turks to the Venetians and the Catholics, who offered feudalism, serfdom and a degree of religious intolerance, although, when it came to the final great siege in the place, at Famagusta, there was another epic of Rhodes-like proportions.

In the mid-sixteenth century, great naval battles took place, as the Ottomans fought the Portuguese in Morocco, the Spanish in Algeria and Tunisia, the Venetians everywhere. This was an extraordinarily expensive business, involving shipping that became obsolete. Galleys were manoeuvrable, and the tactics of battle involved boarding or ramming, both dependent on the seas, and the Mediterranean was not only unpredictable but differed from part to part. The galley slaves – hundreds to a ship – were vulnerable to epidemics, and had to be kept in their quarters over the winter. The galleys had to keep within sight of a shore and could not dispense with land bases for repair and supply. This led to amphibious expeditions against Tripoli or Tunis, themselves at the mercy of sudden storms, such as wrecked not only the Portuguese fleet but the very kingdom itself, which was swallowed by Spain. The whole episode came to an end around 1600 when the Dutch, especially, appeared with tall sailing ships, equipped with artillery that could sweep the seas. But in the later sixteenth century, Islam and Christianity appeared to be fighting for ever and ever.

A climax was reached in 1565. The island of Malta, to which the Knights of St John had repaired, had a strategically commanding position, between Tunisia and Sicily, and it had a deep, long harbour, suitable for the maintenance and supply of ships. Süleyman sent his chief admiral to take the place, and there was an epic battle. It centred upon the fort of St Elmo, commanding the main harbour, which was itself besieged for months, by land, and Malta survived only by a miracle. This finally caused the Spanish to make common cause, in deeds, with the Knights, and the threat of a relief fleet, and the lack of a decent water supply, caused the Turks to withdraw – Süleyman's first real reverse.

But otherwise there was victory upon victory. The Turks had seized the southern Balkans; the Rumanian princes were vassals, paying tribute. To the north lay Hungary, which had fought the Ottomans in the first half of the fifteenth century, sometimes winning battles. Belgrade, known to the Hungarians as 'Nándorfehérvár', was a powerful fortress, protected by a confluence of the Sava and the Danube, and very stoutly constructed; and it had stood out against even Mehmet II in 1456. However, by 1520, Hungary was in decline, as the Crown became an elective one and lost power to a large noble class which oppressed its peasants, and in 1526 Süleyman invaded. At the battle of Mohacs in August that year there was a repeat of the Crusaders' calamitous defeat at Varna in 1444 as stupid chivalry charged Janissaries and guns; quite soon, half of Hungary was in Turkish hands, and the heart of it, the principality of Transylvania, accepted Turkish overlordship.

This turned into a considerable asset for both sides. The Turks gained (as with the Urban who had designed the siege artillery of 1453) some go-ahead people as allies because the schools were very good, and even in 1600 there was a remarkably high rate of literacy. (It reached almost 100 per cent among the Unitarians, for instance, no doubt because, in that oddly talented part of the back of beyond, there were old-established German migrants who had been deliberately chosen, by Hungarian kings three centuries before, for the skills that they could bring.) On their side, the Transylvanians, many of whom had become Protestant, were saved by the Turks from the rigours of the Counter Reformation. On the whole, Transylvania then became a useful Ottoman vassal. Central Hungary fell under Ottoman rule, but in the west and north, there was a different Hungary altogether, in that part of the country which remained under the rule of the Habsburgs, who succeeded the old Hungarian dynasty. Süleyman set up his new capital at Buda, with its Turkish governor, but the frontier remained a matter of dispute, and fighting went on. In 1529 Süleyman briefly crossed it and besieged Vienna itself, but the winter season was approaching, and the Sultan, ever the realist, did not insist.

The long wars on the Habsburg frontier were one thing, and were difficult enough – to muster an army in Hungary meant an enormous effort in logistics, a plod through endless mire, and huge columns of camels carrying supplies, and even cannonballs. The army, halted, would spread out in tents, and those of the Sultan and his retinue were magnificent carpeted affairs (of which a minor variant can still be seen in Central Asia). Given the endless problems, not just on other fronts, but even in a different hemisphere, there were limits to the Ottoman concentration on any one, and in Hungary there were long periods of truce, because the Habsburgs also had other fronts. However, the complications of Central Europe went on and on, and there were intrigues between Vienna, Transylvania and the rulers of the Rumanian lands.

Süleyman grew older and older, more and more set in his ways, and more religious as well. He became less tolerant of the Christians, and took his role as Islamic warrior increasingly seriously. By his last years, Süleyman had become the grandest piece in the fabulous clockwork he himself had devised, and, after the death of Roxelana (also known as Hürrem Sultan), to whom he had been very married, he became ascetic, stern: the court ate off earthenware, whereas it had generally dined from the best Chinese porcelain, some of it given a very thin lining of silver which turned yellow if it came in contact with arsenic. It is not unlike the story of Louis XIV who, in his own way, became a piece of Louis Quatorze Versailles furniture – visited every evening by his mistress, Madame de Maintenon, who talked religion for two hours and then told him to go to bed with the grim, stupid Queen (the two of them cooked up the worst mistake in French history, and expelled the Protestants). Süleyman's relations with his sons (and here Roxelana, as wicked stepmother, has some responsibility) were not good. He had even had one of them murdered, for rebelliousness; that had caused the death, through demoralization, of his brother, Cihangir, who had been Süleyman's favourite. The rest were a job lot and, as so often happens, the spirit of the father went on through the daughter, Mihrimah, whose mosque in Üsküdar is splendid (she has another one, by the wall near the Edirne Gate in Istanbul). One thing the old man knew how to do: battles. In 1566 he mustered his enormous army and moved it northwards, past Belgrade, into Hungary, where, at a fortress, Szigetvár, he started a siege. Then, aged seventy-two, he died.

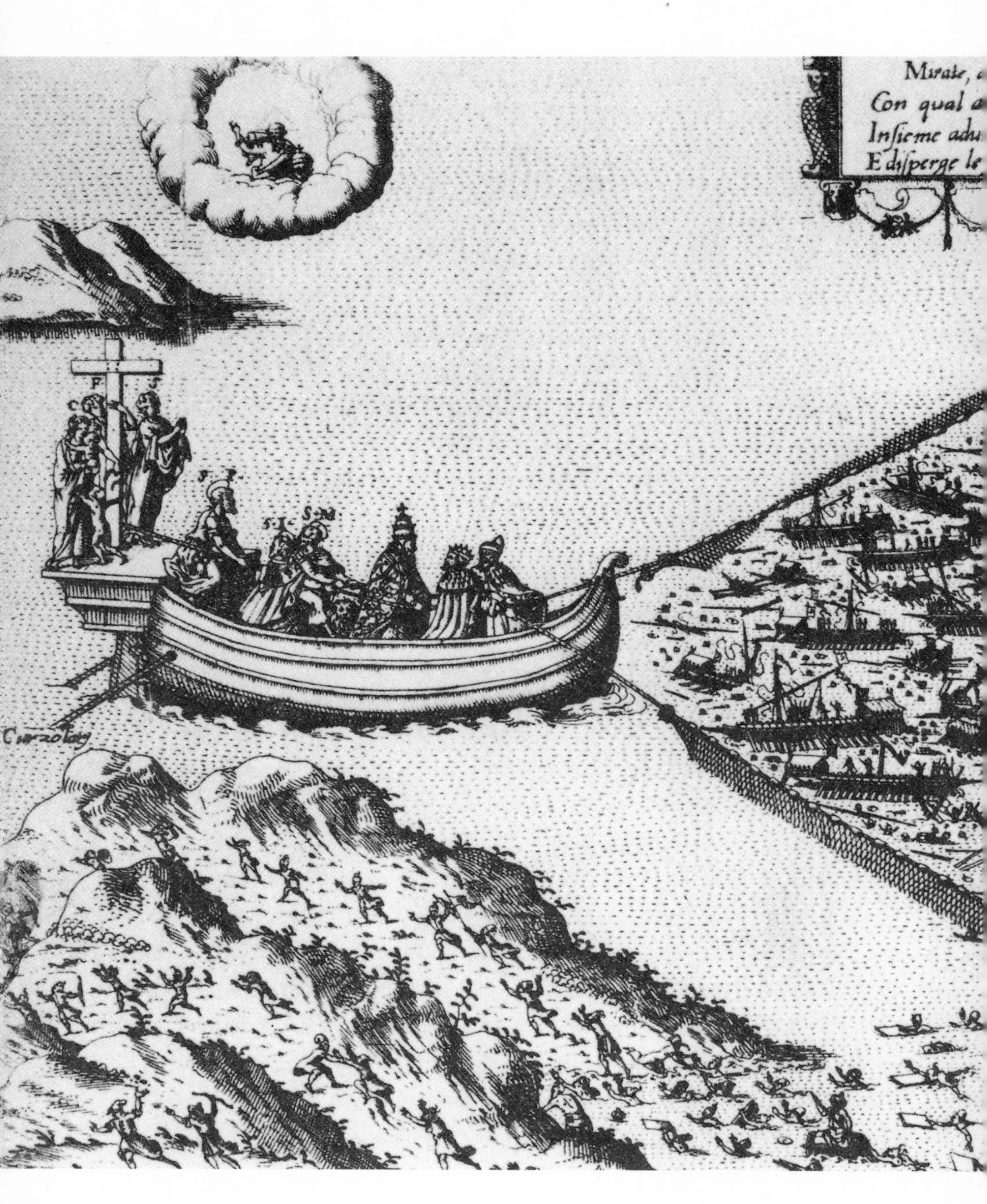
Mirate,
Con qual
Insieme
E disperge

FOUR Shadows

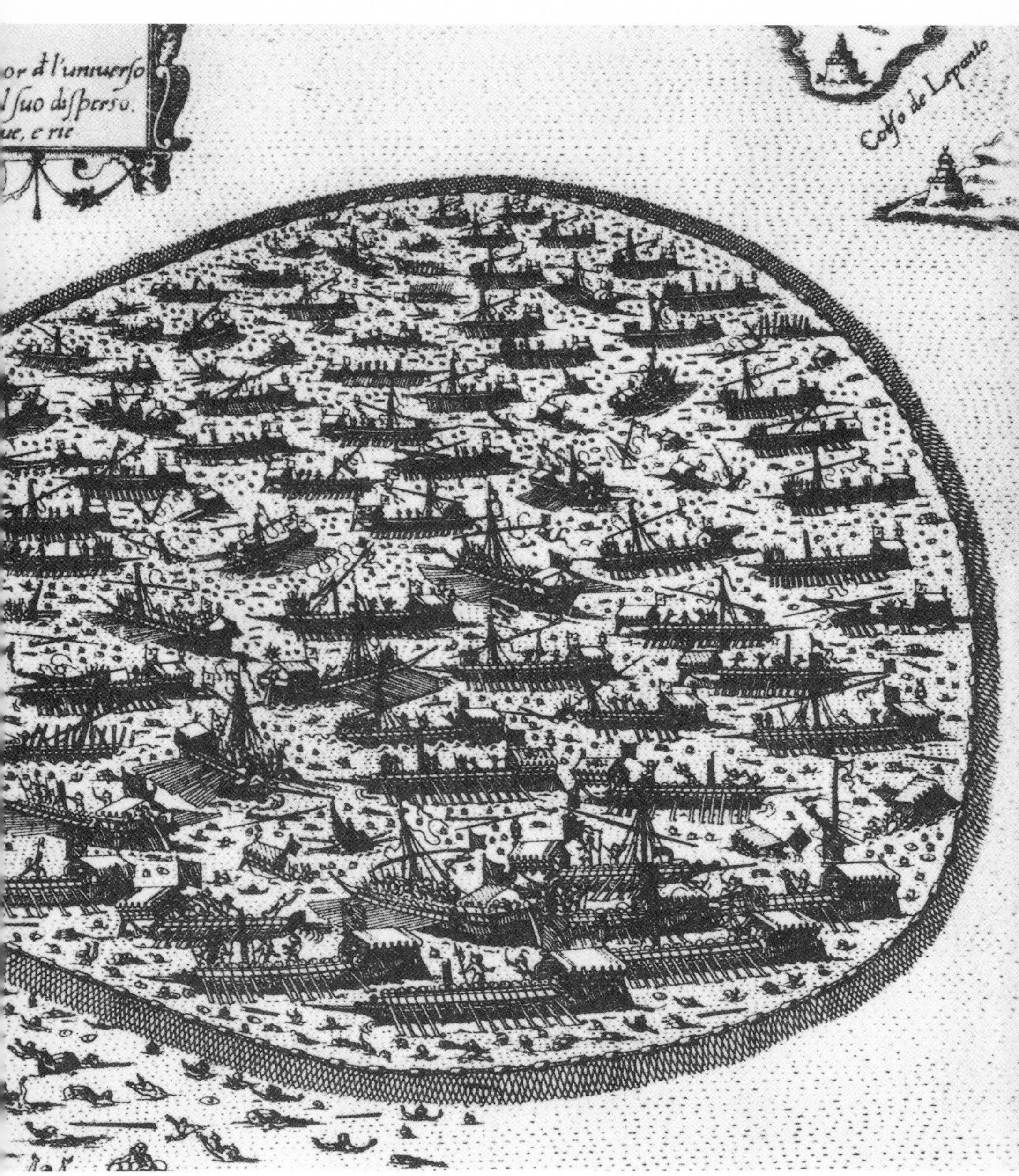

The news of Süleyman's death was kept secret – even for forty-eight days. As ever, this was so that the succession could be smoothly handed over to the candidate favoured by the powers-that-be. But the long-serving grand vizier also feared, as it turned out rightly, that, if the Janissaries knew that there was a new Sultan, they would demand their traditional 'gift', which amounted to a considerable sum. A dummy Sultan was installed in the coach, with pages running alongside, reading the Koran, knowingly taking part in the macabre charade, and the Sultan's body was smuggled back to Constantinople.

By now, the fabulous clockwork went on of its own, and a vizier of genius, Sokollu Mehmet Pasha, arranged the succession to the not unworthy Selim II (r. 1566–74). He enters history as 'Selim the Sot', but whatever his habits, they did not matter, because Süleyman had been acute as regards his choice of grand viziers, the Greek İbrahim Pasha until 1536, when he was executed for becoming too grand, or the enormously tall Bosnian Sokollu Mehmet Pasha, who served three Sultans and died in his bed, though there were rumours that a scheming Safiye Sultan (wife of Murat III) had had him poisoned, because such men knew which switches to use, and they did not include scheming imperial mothers such as Safiye Sultan.

It was in this reign that Cyprus was taken, in 1571. There was a reverse, in the battle of Lepanto, in the same year, when the Spanish and Venetian ships, heavy galleons called galleasses, strong enough to take guns with some range, smashed an Ottoman fleet, and this was presented as a turning point in the Clash of Civilizations, Don John of Austria being the hero of the hour.

The presentation was misleading: Spain and Turkey had more in common than had Spain with England or Turkey with Persia. The Ottomans anyway reconstituted their galleys fast enough (within the year) and went on as before. It was not until 1600 that a real decline could be registered, and it is a decline that affected both sides.

Something went badly wrong with the Mediterranean at that point. It had been the centre of civilization. In the course of the seventeenth century, that centre shifted to the Atlantic. The interesting test case is the Dutch Revolt against Spain, an eighty-years war that ended only in 1648 (when, out of exhaustion, delegates agreed to discuss peace in Westphalia, even then so detesting each other that they met in separate towns, Münster and Osnabrück, communicating through third parties). It was Holland that came up with the things that made the modern world work: national bank, rationally organized military tactics, cleverly designed ships, maritime insurance, a stock exchange, telescopes, agricultural progress that stopped periodic famines. Holland was too small, too fractured, to withstand invasions, and the essentials were transplanted to England by the Dutch, who even took over the throne in 1688. The emerging importance of the Atlantic also lifted off wild and remote Scotland as, fortuitously, Glasgow was the best port for American tobacco, which financed a place that was not used to financing and did quite well out of it.

Historians of Turkey, of Venice, of Spain separately look at the seventeenth century and wonder what went wrong. The decline was universal, though there are so many qualifications that you can, for a time, even debate whether it happened at all. But by 1700, Spain and her empire kept going only because the would-be inheritors could not agree as to partition. Venice was turning into a fabulous Canaletto. Naples had imploded, and Sicily was becoming the world of Giuseppe Tomasi di Lampedusa's *The Leopard* (1958), crafty illiterates baking in baroque ruins. The Ottoman Empire still had a great deal of kick, but it was losing battles, and, over it, there now loomed the shadow of Russia, the last, in a sense, of the great Central Asian empires.

There are various ways of explaining this. A fashionable one, once upon a time, was western imperialism: the arrival of Portuguese, and then Dutch, shipping in the areas of the spice trade. This was a variant of Leninism, to the effect that capitalism was turning into imperialism, and impoverishing the Third World. However, 5,000 Portuguese men and eighty Dutch ships, making a hazardous year-long voyage, were not really enough to topple an entire world system. It was true that the Ottomans lost ground in the spice trade, but the entrepôts at Aleppo and Cairo mainly flourished, and the trade in coffee from the Yemen turned out to be more profitable. It is no doubt true that, in the nineteenth century, an imperialist world system, operated to the great profit of the West, had emerged. Not in the seventeenth. Otherwise, it may be that climate change (and of course the galley wars) led to such extensive deforestation that soil was eroded – an obvious factor on the Ankara plateau. On the other hand, sensible regimes understood how to keep forests going: the main thing was to stop goats. Perhaps that climate change meant new strains of disease, but, again, go-ahead regimes had an idea as to how the plague or malaria or smallpox might be controlled, and for that matter the practice of vaccination had been learned from Turkey. The fact remains that Amsterdam and London had an idea as to how the plague might be isolated and controlled whereas Naples and Constantinople were devastated by it.

The decline of the Mediterranean does offer a field day for critics of religion, whether Counter Reformation Catholicism or Islam, and it is certainly true that both were decorating their intellectual funerals with a grand aesthetic display. The popes did not impress, and there is a good Islamic parallel. The Ottomans, with a large navy, obviously needed to know about the stars, had good map-making, and had installed telescopes on an observatory in the Constantinople district of Beşiktaş (which also suited the Sultans, who took an interest in astrology). There was an earthquake in 1583, and the religious authority made the point that it was God's punishment for these enquiries into His secrets, meaning, probably, that they resented astrologers; the telescopes toppled down, and it was the end of Ottoman naval predominance. Similarly, later on, in the first half of the eighteenth century, religious pressure led to the closure of the schools for mathematics and engineering, and, for that matter, to the restriction of printing. The initiative taken by the enterprising İbrahim Müteferrika was stopped in its tracks by scribes who wanted to keep their monopoly – and calligraphy – and they advanced religious arguments in this cause (although there is also an argument that printed books were simply too expensive for the then very limited reading public). It is no doubt possible to find excuses and exceptions in all of this – there were of course clever clergymen, who shook their heads – but it is rather hard work. By the later eighteenth century, Christian Europe was looking on the Ottomans with the affectionate condescension of Mozart's *Entführung aus dem Serail* (1782).

Still, in the two reigns following Selim II's early death in 1574, those of Murat III (r. 1574–95) and then Mehmet III (r. 1595–1603), the machine worked well enough. The military conquests went ahead: in the 1570s even Morocco, though not for long, became part of the empire, and in the east, as the Safavids faced problems from their own north and east, much of Azerbaijan and Georgia was taken over, though again not for long. Plans went ahead for digging a canal between the Don and the Volga, to enable an Ottoman army from the Sea of Azov to take Astrakhan, on behalf of their allies, the Crimean Tatar Khans (who were able, in 1571, still to reach Moscow and burn it), though the effort proved too great and the Tatars were treacherous. Murat III had already captured the enormous rock fortress overlooking Lake Van, and he had also taken Bitlis, both of them areas with a mixed population of Kurds and Armenians, in the course of his campaign into Iraq; there was an Ottoman presence in Baghdad, where a governor (as it happens, of Genoese origin) tried to maintain the peace between Sunni and Shia Muslims. But in the high mountains of the Anatolian-Iraqi border, control was impossible to maintain. In the end, the decisive defeats for the Ottomans were to happen there. After 1580, there was a considerable Persian recovery, and Baghdad was lost.

By 1580, there was, in the Mediterranean, something of a truce with Venice and Spain, and the Ottomans drew in their horns as far as the Indian Ocean was concerned, but on the northern frontiers, the line held well enough. Again and again, there was local fighting, as bandit-raiders provoked trouble, and this or that Ottoman vassal made surreptitious approaches to the Habsburgs in Vienna. From 1593 to 1606 there was even 'the Long War', mainly consisting of sieges, until both sides composed their differences with the Treaty of Zsitvatorok, each of them having concerns elsewhere, and leaving the line more or less where it had been, in western and northern Hungary. However, in various ways, Süleyman's system was starting to seize up. The first problem was that the empire was too large. There was now a sort of Egyptian-Ottoman partnership and the Egyptian side, the money of which was much needed, had become involved in endless battles – Ethiopia, the Mediterranean – and controlling the Yemen in particular was very difficult, given the terrain and the climate. Then came the Balkans, an endless swapping of blows with the Habsburgs, whether war had been declared or not. Then there was the east, where there were no natural borders, and where the difference between Sunni and Shia Islam made not just for wars in Persia, but rebellion at home. Süleyman had known how to deal with this, and his reign had marked a synthesis of empire: Rome for the law and organization, Islam for the inspiration, Central Asia for the military. The interpretation of these things is problematic, but nowadays the general assumption is that the working models were Persian. His successors were not of the same class, and though the synthesis held for a time, under Süleyman's viziers, in the event the weaknesses came out.

The Ottoman finances had been quite solid, based partly on conquest – especially of Egypt – and partly on taxation. There had of course been problems from time to time, and Mehmet II himself had reduced the silver content of the chief coin, but his conquests and the boom that followed 1453 made up for that. However, now, at the end of the sixteenth century, a mysterious price rise occurred, which disrupted everything. At bottom, there were two causes. The population of the Mediterranean area went up by nearly half (the Ottoman part to maybe 20 million), for reasons which may have to do with the climate change. The region did not produce enough grain to feed itself, and had to import it from the Baltic. There was another cause of the price rise. In South America, the Spanish had hit upon the fabulous silver mines of Potosi (there were other sources, for instance in northern Hungary) and every year the *flota* brought its cargo. Prices then rose, and even the Spanish Crown went bankrupt in 1575 because it could not pay its debts. This process affected the Turks. Venice produced a coin, the silver value of which was unchanging, and everyone therefore used it as a standard.

At the end of the sixteenth century, Turkish coins were again adulterated, but this time the new sources of revenue dried up, and the armies of servants of the state, especially the Janissaries, understood well enough that they were being defrauded. From parity with the Venetian coin, the Ottoman *akçe* dropped by half. The Janissaries, especially, were the brigade of guards, and the symbol of their regiments was a huge cooking pot, meaning that the Sultan kept them going. Their barracks were at the meat market in Aksaray, by the Şehzade Mosque, not far from the Topkapı Palace. Janissaries guarded the palace, and if there were a mutiny, then the mutineers had an obvious advantage. They would move in on the palace, occupy its second court, and demonstratively upset their cooking pot. The only way round this, in the short term, was for a Sultan to offer proper money, and, as early as 1589, there was a Janissary revolt that had to be bought off. That was done, but at the cost of the household cavalry, which then, in turn, rebelled in the provinces (they were prominent in the Celali risings of the early seventeenth century).

In the medium term, the solution was to recruit more Janissaries. The original Janissaries had numbered perhaps 7,000, a real elite of formerly Christian boys who were loyal to each other and the Sultan. The endless wars had made greater recruiting necessary, and since Janissaries had many privileges – in effect, pensions – Muslims were quite anxious to join. Mehmet III allowed this, and the numbers of Janissaries rose to 40,000 and more, a dilution. They were responsible, not just for the civil peace in the capital, but even for firefighting, both of them activities that involved dragooning shopkeepers. The brigade of guards became a protection racket.

An intelligent Sultan would see the extent of the problems, would be presiding over a machinery that produced endless paper (all of it, in millions of documents, preserved in the archives), would have a grand vizier apparently capable of dealing with it all, and would then face the greatest problem in his life, his mother. Western monarchs produced children by some suitable woman, with whom, after the birth of an heir or two, relations were then correct. In the creative period of the Ottoman Empire, something of this sort had been the rule: husband and wife, father and son, father and daughter, had had the usual complicated relationship that nevertheless kept the show on the road. In the later sixteenth century, something went wrong.

One of the Turkish words that have entered the world's dictionary is *harem*. As now understood, it is a misuse. Households were divided between an area open to visitors, the 'greeting area' or *selamlik*, and a private area, called *harem*, where the women of the family could just be themselves. Even the grandest dwellings, including the Topkapı, had the same arrangement. *Harem* has come to signify a sort of revolving grand brothel, but that was not the original meaning at all. Good-looking young girls would be recruited for the service of the court, and given training in various sophisticated matters, such as music or embroidery, or how to talk to a man. The ambitious girls, of course, wanted husbands from the court establishment, and often got them. However, in the later sixteenth century, the custom arose that a girl who pleased the Sultan would have his baby, and if it was a boy, she was kept in privileged circumstances. If her son then became Sultan, she – it is the incarnation of the wicked stepmother – masterminded the execution of his half-brothers, sometimes little boys, to whom the head gardener (this was one of his functions) applied a silken cord. With rope, blood was shed, and by a superstition going back to the old days of the Turks, the soul did not go to heaven. Murat III and Mehmet III (whose nineteen half-brothers, some of them tiny, were killed) could hardly bear the process, and never really recovered. Ahmet I (r. 1603–17) stopped it, and had his half-brothers just kept, meaninglessly, in a rat-infested corner of the *harem*, called the 'Cage'.

However, the victors were the mothers of the Sultans, known as Sultan Valide. They played power strategies with the main figures at court, and these were eunuchs. This was a Byzantine phenomenon, owed to a particular early Christian understanding, not inaccurate, that sex was the work of the Devil. Apparently, the idea goes back to the Copts in Egypt, about whom Gibbon is not respectful (there were monks who, by way of demonstrating whatever, used to crop the grass, like sheep). The great white eunuch, deprived of his testicles, ran most of the palace, including the page boys. The great black eunuch, deprived of everything – you survived the operation, if you did, if you were immediately plunged into hot sand – ran the *harem*. Power-women and eunuchs took over the Ottoman Empire, a chromatic descant on the great themes of Süleyman. With Murat III, the *harem* also acquired the characteristics that we know from caricature. Up until then, the Sultans had made dynastic marriages, with Byzantine princesses, or women from equivalent Muslim families, such as the Girays who ran the Crimea. The *harem* was really a sort of girls' school, equivalent to the institutions that trained the boy pages, and it was only with Murat III that it became at least partly what legend has it to be. Of course, it did nothing to help, as far as the Sultans' characters were concerned, if they were surrounded by a bossy mother and women either sullen or attention-seeking. Most Sultans were figureheads, and they were overshadowed by their own grand viziers.

Up to this point, the Ottoman synthesis had worked. Süleyman had left a governing machine of great effectiveness. There was a truly imperial civil service: from 1453 to 1623, only five out of forty-seven grand viziers were of Turkish origin, as against eleven Albanians and six Greeks (and one Armenian). They were assisted by ordinary viziers, generally four in number, and they presided over an administration that efficiently transmitted revenue to keep the army going (by 1600 the 40,000 Janissaries took a third of the state's wage payments). The grand vizier in effect ran the government, and could amass a fortune (Rüstem Pasha, the second of Süleyman's great viziers, died leaving 1,700 slaves, 2,900 horses and 700,000 gold coins: as son-in-law of the Sultan, he built his own mosque, on the Horn below the Sülemaniye, and it has the outstanding İznik tiles – in this case red – of the city). Up to 100 treasury secretaries kept track of revenue and outgoings, and in the provinces the governors had an equivalent civil service, on a smaller scale. The taxes rolled in, sustaining an army of 200,000 – many more than European states could muster.

A peculiarity was the system by which cavalry was raised. A man got a collection of farms, called *tımar*, and took some of the peasants' output in return for turning up, with six horses, for battle. In that way, there were 80,000 cavalrymen, mustered for service when the first green shoots appeared through the frosts (and disbanded when the autumn had advanced). The *tımar* was given in recognition of a man's deserts, but he might have to give it up at any time, and so a hereditary gentry did not develop: in fact, the empire was an engine for social mobility; Rüstem Pasha, for instance, having started out as a Croat pig-farmer's boy.

The only piece of machinery that was partly out of central control was religious, but even here Süleyman made great inroads. Religion in theory supplied the law – the sharia. A board of senior religious figures, the *ulema*, amounted to a form of supreme court, with a whole set of lesser judges all the way down to small-town level, called *kadis*, who supervised schools and hospitals as well as administering justice. The sharia, a product of the medieval Arab world, hardly fitted modern circumstances, and Süleyman had spent a great deal of his time in drawing up codes of law; he also permitted customary law in the Christian areas.

At any rate, in Süleyman's time, and for a generation beyond, the machinery worked, with the best artillery in Europe, the most courageous infantry, and swarms of cavalry to sweep over the Hungarian plain or the Anatolian plateau. Not only that: there was, internally, much concern for welfare, an anxiety to keep the population of Constantinople reasonably well fed. Prices were quite carefully controlled, and the grand vizier himself would go round the bazaars to detect profiteering. The guilds, officially recognized, set fixed prices, and this explains an otherwise puzzling phenomenon even today, that in certain streets or even quarters, the shops mainly sell the same goods (in Galata, for instance, lamps and musical instruments).

However, it all went wrong. There was for a start the notorious late sixteenth-century price inflation, but its effects were worse because of the debasement of the currency: the fish rotted from the head, and in the early seventeenth century the rot spread. For nearly two decades the Celali revolt made Anatolia ungovernable. But here again was a sign of trouble to come – that the opposition in Turkey was a mirror-image of the government, and equally incapable of providing a serious way forward. The Celalis were a hotch-potch – cavalrymen, their skills obsolete, bandits, religious dissidents, peasants angry at the loss of their land, civil servants angry at the devaluation of their salaries. Ahmet I managed to deal with it, and, to some grumbling, put up the Blue Mosque in celebration. You were not supposed to erect a mosque unless you had had a real and profitable victory. The Blue Mosque has six minarets, an unnecessary display, and is overwhelming, where the Sülemaniye is imposing.

There were other problems, central ones, which the outsider has trouble understanding. Something went wrong with Islam in this period, and not just in Turkey: you can see it at work in India where, in the great days of Akbar, around 1600, Hindus had drunk wine at court, but where, under Aurangzeb fifty years later, intolerance prevailed and a great bout of dynastic civil warring was about to start. One of the pillar institutions of the Ottoman Empire had been the *ulema*, headed by the Sheikh ul-Islam. The court of judges interpreted the religious law, the sharia, which had been handed down by the Prophet but, as Süleyman had found, such law could not possibly cover contemporary conditions and a civil law emerged on the side, interpreted by different lawyers; and the Christians or Jews had their own ways of doing, which were generally respected.

In the Sunni version of Islam, there were four different schools of law. In the Ottoman, Hanafi, variant, you could treat foreigners reasonably well, though the Shafii version, less tolerant, and also more strict as regards women, prevailed in eastern Turkey (you can still see grim old men at Diyarbakır airport in south-eastern Turkey wearing masks to avoid breathing the same air as women and foreigners). Süleyman had wanted the Sheikh ul-Islam to be a sort of pope, capable of decreeing changes in practice when necessary. This did not happen. The religious head of Constantinople, the Mufti, who ranked with the grand vizier, made the clerical and judicial appointments; the result was a lack of central authority, such that, when even a legendary Sheikh ul-Islam, Ebu Suud Efendi, who held office 1545–74, suggested that, after all, interest for bankers might be allowed, he did not prevail. Islam went on officially repeating itself, and in the schools, effort was put into learning the Koran off by heart, which was not an introduction to the modern world.

On top of everything else, Islam in effect splintered. Underneath an appearance of strict unity, with rules even down to such matters as using the left hand for intimate matters, it varied enormously in practice, and especially so in Turkey, where outside influences and old traditions counted for so much. There were brotherhoods – 'sects' would be the wrong word, because there were no theological differences – that reacted against the grim, rule-bound and oppressive world of official Islam. The Bektaşi brotherhood was powerful in the Balkans and among the Janissaries, and took a tolerant attitude towards alcohol. The Mevlevis, the most human one, went back to the great Mevlana (Rumi) of the thirteenth century, who had preached understanding of human weakness and produced the best poetry (they are creators of the Whirling Dervishes). But there were others, the Kadizadelis, making out that, if the empire was not flourishing, this was because the rules of Islam were not being obeyed, and later, reconstruction-minded rulers had to use main force to put them down.

Ahmet I was the last Sultan of the great period, but the tendency now was to apply Islamic rules: otherwise, how, given the Celali revolts and the

Persians' new successes in the east was the country to be controlled? In the early seventeenth century, these ultra-pious men made the running, and the empire became more Islamic. Greek books disappeared from libraries, and nine-tenths of the not many books that were published concerned religion: repetitive, childish stuff, and lives of the saints, as with Counter Reformation Catholicism. Again as with Counter Reformation Catholicism, beggars clustered round the pious foundations, and since these at least were safe from the predatory paws of the state, the rich put their money there, where it did not do anything much. In eighteenth-century Naples, 5 per cent of the entire population consisted of monks and nuns, and the Ottoman Empire also risked turning into an enormous *mezzogiorno*. Increasingly, the productive element consisted of religious minorities and foreigners, protected by their consulates under the rules of what were known as the Capitulations (from the Latin *capita* meaning 'heads of agreement'). The Sharia law, by which the empire was supposedly governed, could not be applied to people with entirely different habits as regards property and, say, banking interest (which was also, theoretically, banned under Counter Reformation Catholicism: monks took over the pawnshops and called them 'Mount of Piety').

When Ahmet I died, a powerful mother emerged as the real ruler. A mentally feeble Mustafa briefly appeared (r. 1617–18), before the Janissaries pushed him back into the 'Cage'. Osman II (r. 1618–22), a young son of Ahmet, took over, with a romantic idea of reform and of leading his troops into battle, this time against the Poles over a Black Sea issue. He knew that the Janissaries had become the problem, and thought of transferring the capital to Cairo. But his campaign on the Black Sea did not go well, the treasury was empty, and the Janissaries, with help from the *ulema*, put Mustafa back on the throne. Osman was humiliated and very cruelly killed, the first deposition of an Ottoman Sultan.

Mustafa was overthrown a year later, and the mother again went into action to install the eleven-year-old Murat IV (r. 1623–40). He started to impose himself when he was only twenty (he died aged twenty-seven) and was a giant of a man, happy leading his troops. If a Sultan had the willpower and ruthlessness, he could control the internal troubles: the essential was finance, cutting back on the innumerable court parasites, and the wages pocketed by Janissaries who did not do any fighting, but instead focused on civilian jobs of one sort or another; extra taxes were raised, and the internal troubles were put down. Murat IV was lucky, in the sense that the Austrians were engaged in the Thirty Years War, and he was able to concentrate against Persia. In 1638, he took back Baghdad – another twist in the Islamic direction. This appeared, also, in other ways. There were laws requiring the various Christians and Jews not to show off: Greeks were supposed to wear blue shoes, Armenians, red, and these laws were for a time enforced. Besides, this Sultan banned alcohol, not a good idea if there is an empire to run. (Ahmet I had even had executed a man caught smoking, and Murat IV executed thousands for this.) He died of disease about a year after his return from Baghdad, and the troubles soon started again.

Murat's successor, his brother İbrahim, was lazy and self-indulgent; he exhausted himself in the *harem* and left matters to his favourites and his mother, who busied herself in palace intrigues with the eunuchs: a caricature of oriental despotism. By now, grand viziers – after all, representing the Sultan in government – could make enormous fortunes, and the only way for a weak man to control them was by a periodic and unpredictable cull, which would also bring down their hangers-on. There were eighteen grand viziers in twelve years – four of them executed, eleven dismissed, two resigning, and only one dying in his bed in office. In 1648 İbrahim himself was deposed and executed (with his mother's consent) and a six-year-old Mehmet IV (r. 1648–87) succeeded – also a Sultan with a powerful mother, who had İbrahim's mother, in the event, strangled.

This was a dismal period, as each change in office meant a new clientele, reaching some way into the entire administration, and matters were made worse because İbrahim frivolously allowed himself to attack Venetian Crete, the source of a very long, expensive and pointless war (which in the end introduced Turkey to olive oil). There had been 60,000 salaried civil servants in 1640; by 1648, there were 100,000, and there was a vast deficit, with Janissary revolts. Besides, the Constantinople mob were enraged, because they were paid in copper money and were expected to pay their taxes in silver, which in 1651 brought about a revolt of the guilds. This chaos caused Mehmet IV's mother to take a creative step. In 1656 she appointed as grand vizier Mehmet Köprülü, a seventy-year-old Albanian, upright and experienced, who accepted the office on condition of a free hand. He and his son Fazıl Ahmet dominated affairs until 1676, after which came another Köprülü, Kara ('Black') Mustafa of Merzifon.

This was a period of recovery, carried out with much harshness. One great problem was that the farms – *tımars* – which were supposed to supply cavalry had been given to non-soldiers, and a forced loan was imposed on them, as well as taxes. The cavalry was purged, with much execution, and loyal troops put down the various rebellions, including one in Egypt. The budget was balanced; Crete was at last won (1669) and on the northern front the situation was stabilized: for a time, the Ottoman Empire was at least nominally in charge of much of the Ukraine. Fazıl Ahmet was as effective as his father had been, and ordered fewer executions; the budget was balanced. The real problem with the Köprülü recovery is that the rule of law was not being established. In seventeenth-century Europe, and especially in England, the rule of law, increasingly, prevailed. But in the Ottoman Empire, property was not at all safe, taxes were arbitrary, and there was seemingly no alternative between tyranny and chaos. Something of a debate goes on as to whether in this period the Ottoman Empire was declining at all. However, in response to this is George Orwell's comment, that war is an unanswerable try-your-strength machine, and only muscle-power wins the jackpot. At least the first two Köprülüs were effective tyrants, and they left monuments, perhaps the last substantial ones: their library, not far from the Grand Bazaar in Istanbul, is a treasure. But there was trouble ahead.

VEUE DU GRAND SERRAIL DE CONSTANTINOPLE
Appartemens des femmes du Grand Sei
Isles des Princes
Sinan kiosc
Caickana ou Remises des Barques du G. S.
Alaik
Partie

FIVE Changing Balance

The Köprülü period had seen an extraordinary extension of Ottoman power into central and eastern Europe, and this was a matter of economics. The empire had not sorted out its financial affairs, except with short-term expedients that would have long-term deleterious effects: confiscations, tax-farms. The trick, yet again, was to rely on the profits of conquest, and if you controlled the bottlenecks of trade, there was money to be had. The Black Sea was still an Ottoman lake, neither Russian nor western European shipping appearing there. The northern shore and the Crimea were run by a functioning Tatar state, under the Giray family, who regarded themselves as very grand, and whose cavalry could move fast over the Ukrainian steppe as, for the Turks, in days of yore. There were complications. Poland, the historic state of the area, was beginning to decompose, much as Hungary had done, and there were romantic outlaws, the Cossacks (the word is Tatar in origin) who escaped any government in sight, and staged formidable raids on horseback in all directions: sometimes they defeated the Poles and at times came to terms with them, as they did with the Turks and the Russians. The Ukraine was lawless and divided, and the Ottoman satellites in Moldavia and Transylvania on the northern border were restive. The whole context was complicated again because Sweden, in the north, was well organized, predatory, and eventually run by a lunatic, Charles XII, and it was further confused because Louis XIV's France was bidding for European hegemony against the Austrian Empire, in alliance with the English and Dutch. Elementary intelligence should have told the Turks to be careful, and it should have warned them against any forward move if the Swedes were dormant and the western Europeans were at peace with each other.

It is a measure of the dream world in which they were living that these considerations did not count. At this time, the rulers of Constantinople did not do their homework. No one spoke foreign languages, and the men who did, generally Christians, were despised and distrusted. Turkish forces had done well against the Poles, had taken up an alliance with some of the Cossacks, and had even laid siege to the great city of south-eastern Poland, Lwów. There were fantasies that the Hungarian Protestants would attract French support (the Turks did not understand that at that very moment Louis XIV was expelling his own Protestants, the Huguenots). At any rate, it was time for a show of force. Kara Mustafa, taking over from Fazıl Ahmet, had delusions of grandeur, and decided to besiege Vienna. Already in 1664 the Austrian army had shown its superior organization in the battle of Szentgotthárd, and a treaty (Vasvár) had followed, enabling the Austrians to concentrate against France in Italy and Germany. Now, in 1683, the Turks denounced the treaty, in a megalomaniac exercise. The Sheikh ul-Islam had warned that the real problem was Russia, but he was waved aside: the empire would play its trump suit, from the top.

An extraordinary logistical effort went ahead, as 200,000 men were marched, more or less at the pace with which guns, manoeuvred across rivers with makeshift bridges and through mud, could proceed – roughly four miles every day on average, all the supplies following, while the grand vizier's silver coach moved through the sludge. This took three months, from Edirne via Belgrade and Buda, where Tatar cavalry and tributary troops from the Rumanian lands appeared. Then the fabulous army, vast tents, treasure and all, assembled before Vienna in July 1683. The bombardment began. However, the cannon shot was carried by camel, and the drawback was that camels could not carry heavy shot. The walls of Vienna had been strengthened, and the shot was too small. It bounced off. The Austrian emperor Leopold had prudently left the city, but he was able to collect allies, and not just allies, but almost every Christian state with an interest in the area, including Russia. Kara Mustafa had chosen his time extraordinarily badly, a moment when the usual wars of France against Austria were in suspense; he managed to unite Poles and Russians against him; the Venetians still had some strength, and they joined in; the dissident Hungarians on his own side were toothless. In September 1683, Polish cavalry and German princes arrived for the relief of Vienna, attacking the besieging army from behind. There was an Ottoman collapse – the army, losing even its tents and its treasure, fled back into Hungary, where Buda soon fell. The defeat at Vienna cost Kara Mustafa his life: he was strangled in Belgrade with a silken cord.

Now came an enormous Christian counterattack, Belgrade fell in 1688 and quite soon the Persians joined in. The Ottoman Empire suffered from its over-extension, and there was a near-rout, the Venetians were back in Greece (it was a Venetian bombardment of Athens that wrecked the Parthenon) and the Austrians in Bulgaria; the Russians advanced on the Black Sea, though the logistics defeated them. In 1687, as the calamities went ahead, there was a mutiny, and Mehmet IV himself was deposed, replaced by a brother, Süleyman II (r. 1687–91), who tottered, bewilderedly, out of the obscure part of the Topkapı, expecting to be executed, and was then informed that he was taking over, as the registrar of the Descendants of the Prophet and the chief officer of the Bearers of the Imperial Flask did their stuff, and the rebellious troops were brought back to loyalty when their leader was given a tax-farm and the governorship of Rumelia. The only real hope lay in the diversion of the Austrians to the west, and this was a longer-term factor that saved the empire again and again.

In 1699 came the Treaty of Karlowitz, by which the Turks gave up Hungary. They would probably have had to give up more, but in 1701 the Habsburgs were sucked into the final great conflict with Louis XIV: the War of Spanish Succession. The battle of Zenta, on the Serbian–Hungarian border, in 1697, had shown how backward were the Ottoman forces, a backwardness reinforced by delusions as to grandeur: the Standard of the Prophet being waved around, encouraging only suicidal attacks. The Ottoman formula was failing and yet, for the moment, there was no other. This was an empire that had to expand, if only to occupy Janissaries who would otherwise make trouble. In the old days it had paid for the Janissaries by conquering some place with some income. Now it was on the defensive, again and again. If the empire were left alone, or if it faced a single adversary, it might survive well enough by the old formulae. Not otherwise. Its only firm hope lay in the rivalry of would-be aggressors among themselves, and, with the War of Spanish Succession lasting until 1713–14, these were duly diverted, and this allowed the Turks to regain some of the lost territory. But when the war ended, the Austrian army, under Prince Eugene of Savoy, was back in the Balkans, defeating an Ottoman army at Peterwardein in 1716, though the Venetians, who had joined in, did less well. They lost part of Greece, but the Treaty of Passarowitz in 1718 brought the Austrians Belgrade, and the Muslim population streamed out of Hungary. The defeats were to some extent made good twenty years later, mainly because the Austrians were involved in war with the rising Prussia; and there was even, for surprisingly long periods, peace: an era (until 1730) known as 'the time of tulips'.

The tulip came from Central Asia, its name from the Persian word for 'turban'; it had been exported from Turkey, and famously there had been a tulip mania in Holland in the 1630s, with absurd speculation in the future price of various bulbs. Now there was a tulip craze in Turkey, fomented by Ahmet III (r. 1703–30), and the flower gives its name to a spectacular, if short, period. Ahmet III was a man of peace, and for once he had had a relatively free upbringing, outside the Topkapı 'Cage'. He was fortunate, in that a new source of revenue was opened up on the Danube from the sale of tax rights, and he spent spectacularly. This was a moment when western and especially French fashions started to penetrate the Ottoman Empire, and Ahmet had a wonderful time with imports or with reproductions: he had his own *köşk* at the palace, where the panelling was covered with various flower-paintings. His ambassador to France came back with glowing descriptions of the parks and palaces at the disposal of the King of France, and Ahmet took over an area at Kağıthane known as 'the sweet waters of Europe', where two streams flowed into the Golden Horn, and there constructed a palace, Sadabad, with elaborate gardens, stocked especially with tulips: there were fabulous ceremonial occasions, complete with tortoises on the backs of which were affixed candles to light up the flowers. For most of this period, there was peace, and 'the tulip time' is affectionately remembered through the miniatures of Levni, the court painter (his images in the *Surname-i Vehbi* of 1720 show the festival of the circumcision of the Sultan's sons, complete with the 'dancing boys' that were a feature of the Ottoman court).

But this was also the last moment of the empire as established by the great Sultans. The Ottomans were going through their paces, and from time to time there were efficient grand viziers – İbrahim Pasha of Nevşehir (in Cappadocia) under Ahmet III especially – who knew that in Europe (and Russia) something formidable had come about. In the first half of the eighteenth century, Ottoman ambassadors established themselves for the first time abroad, in, especially, Paris, and some of them made a serious effort to understand (others were lazy, and dismissed what they saw as infidel antics). Foreign trade grew, and with it a merchant presence in, especially, Smyrna and Salonica; the West itself became fascinated by Turkish fashions and patterns, and relations on a personal level were often very good indeed.

Lady Mary Wortley Montagu (she was the daughter of an earl, and was otherwise very widely connected, especially with Alexander Pope) made one of the classic English contributions to this subject, and she describes, in her letters home, how in 1716 she crossed the frontier of the Ottoman Empire on her way to Constantinople, where her husband had been appointed the British ambassador. At Belgrade, she meets the governor, a man of prodigious energy and charm, who drinks and tells funny stories; but there are bandits round about, and she needs a whole cavalcade of Janissaries to keep her safe on the journey; and the Janissaries maltreat the locals, seeing nothing particularly reprehensible about it. In Constantinople, this wonderful woman observes all sorts of details, and learns the language: she has many Turkish women friends and they tell her a thing or two, not least that, once they are outside the house, veiled, no one knows who they are, so they can have assignations with men, no questions asked.

Nonetheless, it remains true that the Ottoman eighteenth century is the one hardest to understand, because, again and again, you are thrown back on western accounts of it, sometimes of beguiling literary quality, but of course always based on observation from the outside. Once you reach the inside, matters become difficult, for this was a religious age and the Ottoman establishment understood itself in religious terms, with an arcane vocabulary to match. The Sultans succeeded each other, none of them very interesting, and in the case of Osman III (r. 1754–57), a pious bore. On one level, it was all splendid, and everyone noted the extraordinary celebrations, sometimes two weeks in duration, that marked, say, the circumcision of a Sultan's young sons. But there were deep problems, and sometimes these blew up. Ahmet III was overthrown in 1730 by a Janissary revolt, led by an Albanian by name Patrona Halil, who could be silenced only by the execution of İbrahim Pasha and other close associates of the Sultan; in the event, Ahmet's successor, Mahmut I (r. 1730–54), played a long and treacherous game, inviting Patrona Halil and his friends to a banquet, supposedly in honour of their appointments to high places, and then massacring the lot. This was the end of the 'time of tulips'.

The *ulema* continued to interpret the sharia law, making due allowance for contingencies not covered by the Arab God of the seventh century, but the whole show was living on borrowed time. Underneath it all, you can sense a change of mentality. In the first half of the eighteenth century, a great many people seem to have taken the religion fairly lightly, and who knows what was said and done behind closed doors. Even the mosque architecture – the best example being the Nuru Osmaniye, at the Grand Bazaar, and begun by Mahmut I in 1748 – shows rococo influence. His successor, Osman III, tried to restore the religious imperatives – no alcohol and non-Muslims to wear distinctive clothing and so forth – but this was widely ignored, and he did not last long. His successor, Mustafa III (r. 1757–74), was also of no great interest, except perhaps in his being the first to take on a debt. Islam was against debt, but by 1768, as the power of Russia built up, there was not much choice.

The fact was that the imperial system was starting to disintegrate. The Janissaries were all doing something else – shopkeeping if you were lucky, extortion if you were not. Constantinople suffered regularly from great fires that swept through the huddled wooden buildings and, an extraordinary paradox, this theoretically all-powerful regime could not organize town-planning in the style of, say, Vienna, with its broad streets and wide-open spaces, dominated by a noble palace or an elaborate church. The failure to develop great public spaces as in western capitals was because of the sharia law. In all countries there is a contest between the rights of property and the rights of the user of it, and under the sharia law, the users had priority. If they closed off a street and built it up, that was their right, whereas in the western, Roman tradition, the public authorities could organize confiscations of space – or, as in England, the grand aristocracy could have the same effect by use of the wheels and levers of English property law. Not so in Constantinople, or for that matter other Muslim towns, and in this warren, and checked only by conflagrations, disease also spread. Constantinople was notoriously unhealthy. The ambassadors escaped every summer towards the Black Sea, where they had summer houses of some elaboration, generally at Tarabya, the Turkish form of the Greek 'Therapeia', or 'therapy town'. The Sultans themselves often also escaped, in this case to Edirne, where the hunting was good.

In the Ottoman Balkans, the disintegration became serious. In the old days, peasants had been quite well looked after by the imperial officials: they were protected from possible bad barons, their lords. Corrupt or incompetent officials might even be executed, their goods impounded. However, that system had been based on a sort of feudalism, the *tımar*, which had certainly not involved the hereditary ownership that was associated with agricultural capitalism. And the owner could even be removed if he did not carry out his side of the bargain. In the eighteenth century, as commerce spread along the trade route to Salonica, some of these holders began to develop their lands, to bribe local officials, and to turn the land into proper plantation farms, *çiftlik*. This meant a step down for the peasants, a matter complicated again in that, as a vague rule of thumb, the big farmers were Muslim and the peasants, *reaya* or 'flock', generally Christian. It mattered again that the lands of the Orthodox Church, which were badly run, were extensive; the result was a peasantry with less and less land, that land often rocky and poor.

Banditry then resulted all over the Balkans, and especially in mountain areas. In Greek these men were known as *klephts* and they were often celebrated, in saga and song, as Robin Hoods. What were the estate owners to do? They recruited other bad-hats, as policemen, and these were called *armatoles*. A brilliant French historian, Gilles Veinstein, describes this as a move 'from bandit hero to burglar gendarme', and that fits. The Balkans were becoming ungovernable, and from time to time there would be savage reprisals – you went along some appallingly difficult muddy road, and you would come across some tall poles, at the top of which, writhing, would be men agonizing from impalement. Already, by 1770, bright sparks in the Balkans might wonder whether progress could arrive from the West.

However, such intelligence was not prominent at the court of Mustafa III. No one knew anything in any depth, and sometimes even on the surface, of the great emerging power, which was the Russia of Catherine the Great. There were old connections with Poland, which was overrated, and with Sweden. Venice was now toothless, and Austria had her face turned towards Germany; France was friendly. In the grip of delusion, Mustafa III allowed himself to be sucked into war with Russia, essentially over the Black Sea. The Russians had been probing the northern Caucasus, over which there was theoretical Ottoman sway, and they were taking overt interest in the Crimea, an Ottoman vassal-state. The rulers of Moldavia, adjoining the Ukraine, had obviously been intriguing in St Petersburg. Mustafa III would show who was master of the Black Sea, and he went to war with Catherine in 1768. All of a sudden, the brilliant façade of the eighteenth-century Ottoman Empire was about to collapse.

SIX The Long Defensive

A Turkish saying goes: one disaster is better than a thousand pieces of advice. The six years' Russian war of 1768 was such a disaster, and it ended with the Treaty of Küçük Kaynarca in 1774. Here, the vital thing was not so much the loss of territory as of prestige and of money; the myth of empire imploded. The Black Sea had been an Ottoman lake more or less since 1453, and there were taxes to be had from traders moving their goods down the Danube from Central Europe or the Dnestr and Dnepr from Russia. The Crimea, with a very mixed population, was the heart of the Tatar state, under the Giray dynasty who, claiming to be the senior descendants of Genghis Khan, had also accepted Ottoman suzerainty; there were other Tatars who took the Russian side, especially the Nogay in the northern Caucasus (they were eventually used to control revolutionary Russian mobs, and their long whip, the *nagayka*, commemorates their existence in revolutionary iconography). The northern Caucasus was, in theory, Turkish, in that the Circassians who lived in the western part of it were, again mainly in theory, Muslim – tough mountain tribes. In the Caucasus, the Turks and their allies fought hard enough, but in the Balkans, in the Danube delta, the results were dismal.

It was at sea, especially, that the empire met its disastrous moment. In the Mediterranean, a Russian fleet appeared, including some British naval staff – characteristic of the creative way in which Russia was using her foreigners. This began, of course, with the empress herself, who had come from a subdivision of Anhalt, a German principality the size of a decent golf course, and who had taken the throne in 1762 by getting her lover to bash out her husband's brains with a footstool. That man, Peter III, upon succeeding to the throne six months' earlier, after the death of his aunt, Empress Elizabeth, had appeared quite drunk at the requiem service, and had ordered the substitution of a Te Deum. But now these northern barbarians put an end to the Ottoman monopoly of the Black Sea. Their fleet sailed altogether by surprise towards Ottoman Greece, where officers landed and tried to bring about an Orthodox rebellion, and then towards the port of Smyrna, and in 1770 smashed an Ottoman fleet to pieces at Çeşme, near Chios, with a combination of fireships and superior seamanship. It was characteristic of the state of Ottoman intelligence that no one could work out how the Russians had got there in the first place: was there not some river called the Rhine, running through Europe?

At this point, we can start referring to the chief government office in Constantinople, the *Bab-ı Ali*, the Gate of the Exalted State, as its central place of decision, and in a French shorthand that became universally used, this becomes 'the Porte'. When the war ended in 1774, the Porte had to accept the loss of the Black Sea monopoly. Russia became the dominant power in the northern Caucasus and was on the way to taking over Georgia. The Crimea had independence devised for it, and one of the Girays, Şahin, by all accounts a very handsome young man, became Catherine's lover. Another Giray converted to Scottish Protestantism, fell in love with a Miss Patterson from Edinburgh, and eloped with her when her (lawyer) father said he was not having his daughter married to an Oriental even if he was a prince; she was still in her palace in the Crimea when the British army landed fifty years later, and had a descendant who, marrying a von Gersdorff, had the last society wedding in Nazi Germany. The Crimean and Nogay Tatars then fought among themselves and in 1783 Russia annexed the Crimea straight-out. The only thing that the Sultan could do was to say that he should be recognized as protector of the Muslims, to which Catherine the Great agreed, on condition that she also became protector, in some vague way, of the Christians in the Ottoman Empire, a matter that constituted a long fuse.

With Russian ships (some of them Greek, using a flag of convenience) now sailing through the Bosphorus, with Tatars and Circassians arriving as refugees in Anatolia, with the loss, for the first time, of territory that had been Muslim, there was a crisis in the state. Of course, intelligent people had been saying for years that things had to change, but they had got almost nowhere, because the system, in its own way, did work, and there was very little pressure for change from within. Even the Orthodox Church was quite satisfied, and it certainly did not want outsiders enquiring as to its doings (at the time, German visitors to Mount Athos found that Byzantine manuscripts were being used to prop a door open, or even just to heat stoves). The thousands of Janissaries uselessly drew their state money and often sold off their entitlement deeds to Armenian speculators. The Sultan could really only run what was called 'Hüdavendigar', in effect the very early Ottoman region round Bursa, though of course now including Constantinople (this area still accounts for about two-thirds of the Turkish GDP).

Elsewhere, local chieftains ruled, without much reference to the Sultan. North Africa had long gone, except as a fictional dependency, although the descendants of the Janissaries, and their local women, were still powerful and, in the name Köloğlu, have an advantage in modern Turkish affairs. The Egyptians were barely under control, and the Arabs of Syria or Iraq had their own potentate-operated tax-farms, paying the state the small change and then milking the locals. The worst such case occurred in the Rumanian lands, Wallachia and Moldavia. There, the native dynasties had, with some help, died out. The thrones, and the tax rights, were then auctioned off every year among the rich Greeks of the Fener quarter in Constantinople, living in elaborate houses clustered round the Orthodox Patriarchate. One after another, the Soutzous, the Ghikas (of Albanian origin), the Mavrocordatos, would arrive in the Wallachian capital, then at Craiova, with their relatives and a bodyguard of Albanians bearing large empty chests. A proclamation would then declare the reign well and truly open, and associate this with taxes, whereupon the peasantry would disappear, leaving belongings to be impounded, after which another Greek would arrive, perhaps called Prince Ghika XIV, and do the same. As time went by, consciences were struck, and in the fourth generation these Ghikas and Soutzous became liberal nationalists, noting the (overdone) Latin origins of the Rumanian language and referring to themselves as cousins of the French.

Where, in all of this, do you start? What struck the powers-that-be after the Treaty of Küçük Kaynarca was the extraordinary success of Russian arms. The first step was therefore military reform, and, here, the great obstacle was the Janissaries. They could not be abolished, and there was not much money to buy them out. Sultan Abdülhamit I (r. 1774–89) had taken over from the discredited Mustafa III and you can see a brain working. There would have to be some sort of new army, and it would have to learn from the West. The French were the most useful of the foreigners, and they were known to have good artillery. Earlier, there had indeed been western experts, but they had not really got anywhere, because religious conservatism, or perhaps plain resentment of know-it-all foreigners, had blocked their path. Even when, as the best one (Humbaracı Ahmet Pasha) did, they converted, they were dismissed as mere opportunists.

Now, an artillery expert did arrive, yet another of the Hungarians, the Baron de Tott (probably a Slovak – *Tót* is a nasty word for that, in Hungarian, the equivalent of 'nigger'), though he came on French say-so. He installed a corps of bombardiers, trained them well, and then ran into the ancillary problems. Artillery was not just about loading guns: you needed decent mathematics, and the *ulema* had closed down the school of mathematics fifty years before, on the grounds that it was probing secrets best left to the Devil. Or so the story runs; we may doubt it, for the Turks, like the Russians, have an excellent mathematical tradition, and they have made the leap into computer-civilization very successfully indeed. However, the Baron de Tott, with four superbly readable though maybe highly embellished volumes of memoirs, had only his corps of bombardiers to show at the end, and the Janissaries did not like it.

In 1787, hoping to take back the Crimea, the Ottomans declared war, again, on Russia – after an absurd miscalculation that the Swedes, then also attacking Russia, would have weight to pull. As things turned out, the Russians could not concentrate against Turkey, partly because of Swedish attacks but mainly because they were diverted by Polish matters and by the French Revolution. There were even Turkish victories in the Caucasus, but these achieved nothing, because the Austrians joined their Russian ally, and re-took Belgrade, although, with concerns as regards France, they gave it back. This meaningless war was otherwise distinguished by one of those episodes that reveal the problems of development. The Baron de Tott had not done badly at all, but the resources for proper artillery were lacking. Do you then opt for some spectacular big gun, or for several smaller ones? The Ottomans opted for the big gun, and fired it from the fortress of Ochakov, at the mouth of the Dnepr. A great shell went into the air, and split into countless fragments, also destroying the gun. Ochakov fell. Such episodes made for ill-tempered debate in Constantinople: was it that foreigners were treacherous, or that more foreigners were needed, with a deeper programme?

Abdülhamit I died in 1789 and was succeeded by an enterprising nephew, Selim III (r. 1789–1807). It is with him that the conscious westernization of Turkey begins. He had to confront the opening of what was to become known as the Eastern Question. It is simple enough, and remains with us: what happens when Turkey goes? Everything was involved: strategy, economy, religion. Might Orthodox Russia remake a Byzantine empire based again at Constantinople? For this, her alliance varied between England and France, with either of which she might manage a partition. In 1798 the question was first put on the table: Napoleon landed in Egypt.

The outstanding history of Germany (by Thomas Nipperdey) begins with the sentence, 'In the beginning was Napoleon', because he it was who shook up the old Holy Roman Empire from top to bottom and started Germany on her modern course, a sort of exported Thirty Years War. Napoleon in a way had the same effect in Spain: the Peninsular War, from the Spanish (not British) perspective, was the start of a long civil war, still not entirely resolved. In the Turkish Empire, as it was then known, something of a civil war also started at this time, between modernizers and conservatives, and it too is still, in a way, with us. The Revolution of 1789 had given France enormous energy, and by 1797 she had made conquests that went far beyond those of the old regime: there were satellite states in Germany, Italy, including the old Venetian empire, which was taken over, as were the Low Countries, Belgium and Holland. The new revolutionary regime, Napoleon its outstanding general, took up an idea of its feeble predecessor. France had lost India and America to the British. Why not make up for that with a far greater prize, the Levant or Near East? Besides – at any rate for dreamers spinning globes in Paris – occupation of that area would allow France to threaten the British in India, whether by crossing a potentially allied Persia, or even by digging a canal from Suez to the Red Sea, suitable for warships.

In July 1798, Napoleon, then twenty-eight, with a sort of pharaonic panache, smuggled an army past the British navy and landed it in Egypt. He put the Mameluke aristocracy, all charging camels and whirling sabres, to flight, and the brightest of them realized that here was something else, a relief from the dozy tyranny of the Turks. The first year or so did not go badly, although the French were bottled up because, when the British, under a Nelson who also had his share of panache, finally found the French fleet, they smashed it to bits. Napoleon then marched into Turkish territory, suffered something of a reverse, and blotted his reputation by ordering a massacre of prisoners. In 1799, recognizing that he had lost the gamble, he smuggled himself back to France, and soon took over. But he had opened up the Eastern Question, and he also launched Egypt on an interesting course: westernization. Quite consciously, using native Egyptians and French officers who had stayed on, a creative figure emerged there, one Mehmet Ali.

He was an Albanian by origin (and all his life spoke Ottoman Turkish). He created quite a serviceable army and navy; he got foreign experts to develop industries; he invaded Arabia and controlled the fanatical Wahhabi sect that had arisen there. There was nothing much that Selim III could do against him, so he was given recognition as a viceroy – in fact, sovereign of a new Egypt. You might even argue that, in this period, the creativity came from Egypt, as the Turkish historian Şerif Mardin suggests, whereas the dead weight was Baghdad. Selim, meanwhile, faced attacks from the British in 1807 (they were repelled because the French ambassador galvanized the defences of the capital) and also found himself at war with Russia. It was something of a non-war, because Selim's own troops, the Janissaries, were too busy running their protection rackets to turn up at the front – only half a dozen out of every regiment. But in 1812 Napoleon attacked Russia, and peace was made with Turkey, which forfeited a valuable stretch of territory along the Black Sea coast, north of the upper part of the Danube delta, called southern Bessarabia (in Turkish, *Bucak*, meaning 'corner'). It mattered, because of ports through which trade entered the Black Sea from Central Europe, and the Austrians, though giving priority to the great port of Trieste, were also interested in this Danubian route. Turkey was being dragged into the world of western capitalism, and how should she respond? India and China faced the same problem, and both collapsed.

Selim III had indeed built up a new army, in a certain sort of stealth, at barracks on the Asian side of the Bosphorus, and there he trained soldiers in imitation of Mehmet Ali. However, his problems were far greater than the ruler of Egypt's. In the eighteenth century, local chieftains, whether in the Balkans or in Anatolia, had acquired the tax rights sold by the Sultans, and these warlords then ignored the central authority. With private armies, they ran fiefdoms – the greatest, that of Ali Pasha of Tepedelen, in the mountain country of southern Albania and north-western Greece, the Epirus. Lord Byron visited, fascinated by the exotic power on display – the huge cushions, the carpets, the water-pipes, the girls, the boys (which caused some muttering among British officials later on, who thought that the Turks took up boys because they were bored by polygamy) – and Ali Pasha's fictional daughter is heroine of Dumas *père*'s *Count of Monte Cristo*, 'la belle Haydée'.

There was another such huge fiefdom in the south-eastern Balkans, the territory known as Rumelia, not far from the capital itself.

Selim III tried to use local Janissary regiments to control these chieftains, and then vice versa, and the whole effort fell apart. In 1807 he was deposed, and a feeble-witted Mustafa took his place; the New Army was disbanded; then a clever grand vizier, using support from the *ulema* and others who detested the Janissary bullies, organized the overthrow of Mustafa; whereupon the Janissaries murdered Selim, whose place was taken by his very young half-brother, Mahmut II (r. 1808–39). He was to play a very long game: in its way, the might-have-been of the later empire.

The Janissaries, marauding in Constantinople and other towns – even in Syria – had other things to think about, and Mahmut, well advised, was very careful. The New Army was reconstituted in an unprovocative way. An overall conference was held with the local potentates, and an agreement as to progress was arranged (most of them, fearing assassination at a banquet, did not appear, and the agreement was not honoured, but it served to give them an idea of the Sultan's weakness). Matters ticked over, and foreign officers came to help train the New Army. This is really the start of a new Turkey.

Armies and modernization are a good subject. In the Atlantic world, to which progress had now shifted, armies were a tool, and not an inspiration. Outside the Atlantic world, where progress was at the mercy of obscurantist clerical institutions and backward local potentates, armies offered the best means for modernization; in Russia or Austria (or even Louis XV's France) if you wanted modern schools, you used the army. The best school in Vienna was the cadets' Theresianum and so it was with the 'Junker institutions' in Russia, or the military schools in Berlin, where so many of the writers, including Leo Tolstoy and Heinrich von Kleist, were educated. The Prussian Helmuth von Moltke, architect of the victory over France in 1870, was also author of a literary classic, his letters from Turkey, where, in the 1830s, he was a foreign military adviser. There was another instance of this phenomenon in the Low Countries, after the French revolutionary armies won the battle of

Fleurus in 1794. They occupied the great university of Louvain, where, in clouds of chalk dust, students solemnly discussed, in Latin, whether Adam and Eve talked to each other in the polite form or familiarly. The French stabled their horses in the precincts, exiled the rector to Guiana, and turned the whole place into a school for medicine and engineering. Modern Turkey was eventually to be made by the army, in a not dissimilar way.

Still, before progress could happen, there had to be disasters, and these duly came about. Egypt was already for practical purposes independent. Once the Napoleonic Wars came to an end in 1815, troubles broke out in the Balkans. Earlier, in 1804, there had been a revolt in Serbia, where one 'Black George' had for a time managed to set himself up as prince, and after a decade of warring, a small Serbia emerged, under another prince who cunningly accepted the Sultan as sovereign. To outsiders, this might seem to be a Christian people emancipating itself from the tyranny of the Turk. Insiders knew there was much more to it: Black George had been encouraged by the Russians when they were at war with Turkey, and then discouraged when they were at war with the French. In any case, he was used by the Sultan's officials to do down the local Janissaries. However, almost none of these alleged movements of national liberation is what it purports to be, and this was borne out by the next, and easily most dramatic, of them: Greece.

The Greeks had really run a sort of empire within an empire, were all over the Balkans and the Near East, and had been since the very start of the Ottoman state. The Orthodox Patriarch was the greatest landowner in the empire, and that office was highly contested (between 1453 and 1918, only four of the Patriarchs died in office, in their beds). The port of Smyrna, dominated by Greeks and Levantines, had become a vital part of the Mediterranean trading network, and the great island of Chios, very close to it, was also a considerable commercial centre. Its merchants were truly international: they were Catholics, sometimes with names that were half-Italian and half-Greek, such as Calvocoressi or Mavrocordato, and they spoke a mixture of Italian and Greek called 'frangochiotike'. In the later eighteenth century, they started to establish themselves in London.

Catherine the Great had had the idea of raising the banner of Orthodoxy in 1770 in the Morea (so called from a word meaning 'mulberry') or, in the classical expression, the Peloponnese, which had once contained Sparta, and Russian officers had landed, to make trouble, but they had got nowhere. Now, with the involvement of France and Russia in the eastern Mediterranean, change was obviously coming, and at one stage the Russians even occupied the seven Ionian Islands (the largest, Corfu) off the Greek west coast. They had been Venetian, and Venice, in 1797, had been abolished. In the troubles of the eighteenth-century Ottoman Empire, there had been one success story: Greek merchants and shipping, expertly conveying goods through Trieste from Central Europe and via Odessa from Russia, whether to Salonica or Smyrna. The merchants had masonic connections in London, and a secret society modelled on the Freemasons got going; among the rich Greeks of the Fener quarter in Constantinople, there were sympathizers. With Russian connivance, some Greek nationalists under a Prince Ypsilanti went over the river Prut into Moldavia in 1821, hoping to bring about a rising: at that time, Greeks ran the upper elements of the church, even in the Rumanian lands, and of course constituted much of the merchant class and the aristocracy. That revolt failed: the local Rumanian peasants preferred the Turks to the Greeks. But another revolt broke out in the Morea; a clergyman proclaimed the rising, and organized a gruesome killing of the entire Muslim population of Corinth, including women and children, as, with a cease-fire and a safe-passage organized by the British, they tried to leave.

Word of this atrocity reached Constantinople, and retribution was swift. The first absurd mistake was to hang the Patriarch, who had been pronouncing anathema against the rebels, and a good twenty other prominent Phanariots (from the Fener quarter). The next mistake was to massacre the inhabitants of the wrong island. Chios had been entirely loyal. The next-door island,

Samos, which produced only pirates and a thin red wine, hated Chios, and in March 1822, at dead of night, Greeks from there landed and pushed a few harmless *zaptiyes* (constables) into the sea. Word got back to Smyrna, where the governor, one Karaosmanoğlu, ordered retribution. On Chios, this happened, and it might be described as the first Turkish public-relations disaster. Delacroix painted a painting, all raped virgins, villainous Asiatics, and so on. The European Romantics became worked up.

The greatest of them all was George Gordon, Lord Byron. The poet was in his mid-thirties, and, in the Adriatic, was running out of inspiration and money. He was bored of his then mistress, one Teresa, and sent her back to her aged husband in Ravenna. He would show the world that he was not finished, yet, and this is the start of a long process, by which western writers turn up in odd places to stand on barricades and say *no pasarán*. Byron appeared at Missolonghi, in the Gulf of Corinth, and fell in love with a boy, one Loukas, who screeched and screamed until he was given a coat of gold in which to sit upon his donkey, while his relatives politely removed Byron's money. Our romantic poet then turned his face to the wall and died, the first martyr of Greek independence. He had said it himself, in his poem *Lara*: 'In self-inflicted penance of a breast/ Which tenderness might once have wrung from rest;/ In vigilance of grief that would compel/ The soul to hate for having lov'd too well.' He did not add another of his lines, about 'the unwonted faggots' hospitable blaze'. If the Turks had Byron and Delacroix against them, they would have quite a fight. The young William Ewart Gladstone was, at the time, reading it all up.

These people had a romantic idea of Greece, as opposed to the classical Rome that had inspired the French in the seventeenth century. It was partly a German nationalist reaction to the domination of the French, and this explains the extraordinary structure of old German sentences, verbs at the end, and relative clauses turned into a lengthy adjectival phrase with a participle before the noun. Nowadays, Germans brought up on *Der Spiegel* cannot easily follow it, and in Berlin Kant is taught in English. Northern

Europe went mad for Hellas, and, post-Napoleon, there were various out of work military men who could be hired, and the Greek merchants had money: Calvocoressis and Mavrocordatos mixed in masonic circles in London, Paris and St Petersburg. The worst thing that the Turks had done was to alienate them, for these were not enemies to make, the more so as some of them, like the Vorontsovs from Russia, married high in England. Being anti-Turkish became 'tone'. There was of course more than a degree of humbug – good old English word – about this. When it came to atrocities, the Greeks gave as good as they got. Somehow, then and later, the Muslim victims were forgotten, and the Greeks were practised hands at image-management, whereas the Turks, *horresco referens*, were not. Again and again they were driven onto the defensive, saying that the numbers were exaggerated and that anyway it had been their fault. It was also true that, despite their support of Greek independence, the Powers knew only too well that the end of the Ottoman Empire would bring problems, as indeed happened. Metternich of Austria, the outspoken reactionary, had no illusions: Greece, he said, was condemned to life.

Much of the nationalist legend was bogus. Byzantium had really been destroyed by the Italians, not the Turks who, if anything, had saved it. Ancient Greece had been destroyed by Celts, after Alexander, and then she had been destroyed all over again by Slavs in the eighth century. She had been re-hellenized by the Byzantines, and Greek nationalists could never agree as to whether they were Hellenes or – clerically – Byzantines. The peasant Greeks talked a very corrupted form of the language, which had been preserved in the churches; and besides, much of the peninsula was honeycombed by Vlachs, shepherds related to the Rumanians, or Albanians, who, mainly, occupied what was left of Athens. Quite soon, the Greek revolt developed into a civil war, rival teams of bandits slugging it out, and it was only really at sea that the rebels had the advantage, because they were much better sailors than the Turks, who could not properly manage a bombardment in the swelling seas of the Aegean: shots went too high, into the sky, or too low, into the sea. On land, there was a sort of mobile impasse. The pattern was for the Turks to come down from the north in the campaigning season, which caused the Greeks to suspend their quarrels, only to start them again when the Turks had to go away as winter approached.

In 1826, there was a sudden change. Mehmet Ali, from Egypt, had sent his son, İbrahim Pasha, with an army and a navy, and these began to put down the revolt. The Romantics became agitated. At that point, the Russians started to make trouble, as they had their own designs in the Balkans and, especially, the Caucasus, where they were already at war with Persia. How were the British and French to keep a balance in the eastern Mediterranean? They teamed up with the Russians, and the three fleets arrived off the Peloponnese to try and separate the combatants. In 1827, at Navarino Bay, someone fired a shot; İbrahim's fleet was smashed to pieces. Then, in 1828, safe from Allied intervention against him, Tsar Nicholas I attacked Turkey, hardly in any condition to defend herself. She duly collapsed and sued for peace, giving Russia control of the eastern coast of the Black Sea; and in 1832 the Ottomans accepted the independence of a very small kingdom of Greece, for which a junior German was selected as monarch. This new state consisted mostly of the barren Peloponnese, the ruins of Athens (there were Byzantine churches on the Acropolis) and some of the islands. It was very poor, and for much of the nineteenth century its inhabitants migrated, if they could, to much more prosperous western Anatolia.

For the Ottomans, the independence of Greece was, nonetheless, a shock to the system. There came another one. Mehmet Ali had by now set up in considerable state, and he had excellent relations with the French, who wanted to use him to extend their own dominion in the Near East. Mehmet Ali himself had ambitions to take over Syria; after all, the rulers of Egypt, before the conquests of Selim I, had advanced far into Anatolia itself. The south-eastern part, adjoining Syria, had once been the Roman province of Cilicia: Campestris, the plain, was (and is) rich in cotton, and Tracheia, the mountainous or wild part, had great strategic value. Mehmet Ali bargained with Mahmut II, and in 1831, sure of French support, invaded. Again, Mahmut II's army failed, and Egyptian troops threatened Constantinople. This presented the Russians with a problem that they never quite managed to resolve. Turkey was supposed to be the hereditary foe. Now she risked being taken over by a French ally: so she would have to be defended. Russian troops therefore encamped outside Constantinople, this time as protectors of the Turks, and this was allowed under a treaty of 1833, Hünkâr İskelesi. Mehmet Ali went away, resolved to try again. In 1839, he did, and again won, but this time the British also had a hand in stopping him, because they too did not want the French controlling Constantinople, and the Levant in general. There was a reason for this: the Ottoman Empire had been falling under British influence as Sultan Mahmut II sought to stem the decline and to launch the empire on a process of reform.

The Sultan had waited, all through the years of the Greek revolt, the Russian war and the initial crises with Egypt. He needed time to train the New Army, and even to recruit Janissaries to it who were willing to change their ways. The population of Constantinople, and especially the guild members who hated the Janissaries' protection rackets, needed to be on his side, and so did those parts of the *ulema* (in effect a civil service) who were not in league with the Janissaries. There was a religious dimension to this. Sunni clerics did not like the Bektaşi brotherhood, with its free-and-easy ways as regards rules (and, for that matter, its appropriation of religious revenues), and the Janissaries' own religion now centred upon the Bektaşis. Meanwhile, these alleged soldiers went on being parasitical, drawing a wage-ticket – sometimes, 120,000 in a year – that guaranteed state money and could even be sold to some Armenian dealer, though at a discount.

In 1826 the time came for Mahmut II to deal with the problem, and, with great cunning and careful timing, he provoked trouble. The Janissaries fell into his trap, and mutinied. The mutineers made an absurd mistake, abandoning the central area of Constantinople around the Hippodrome and the Topkapı Palace, and returned to their barracks on what is now the grounds of Istanbul University, where they staged the traditional ceremony of overturning their cooking pots. One of their one-time leaders, who had gone round to Mahmut's side, approached the barracks with a view to a parlay. He got nowhere. The Sultan's men then brought up cannon, shot the front gate to pieces, went on bombarding until thousands of Janissaries had either fled or been slaughtered, after which mobs went around the city, hunting out the fugitives. Some of them escaped to the provinces, or hid out in the Belgrade forest, north of the city towards the Black Sea coast; the Bektaşi brotherhood was banned (and reconstituted, oddly enough, by the supposedly reactionary Abdülhamit II much later). This destruction of the Janissaries was called the Auspicious Event, or *Vaka-i Hayriye*, and Mahmut put up an elaborate, almost rococo, mosque on the waterfront of the Bosphorus, near the Tophane arsenal, in celebration. It is called the Nusretiye, meaning 'victory'. So it was, and a new army did indeed come about, though it was not strong enough to fend off Mehmet Ali when the time came. In fact Mahmut II, who had begun to drink heavily, died in 1839 just in time not to hear the news of the second victorious irruption of the Egyptians at Nizip. His son Abdülmecit took over (r. 1839–61).

Abdülmecit had been given quite a serious European education, and, in the circumstances of 1839, this fitted, because Europeanization, thanks to his father, had got under way. Mahmut II had for a start changed the official dress, now that the empire was part of the European system: no more kaftans and turbans. Mahmut suddenly appeared, like his troops, in trousers, and a long coat was designed, the *stambouline*, buttoned at the neck. In the late 1820s he decreed that his subjects were to wear, not the turban, but new headgear, the fez. It was a convenient conical cap, apparently Christian and seafaring in origin, which had the advantage that its wearer could bow down in prayer and not knock his hat off when he hit the floor. It had a tassle on top, the story being that the wearer could be yanked thereby to heaven. The fez also had the benefit that it could be worn by non-Muslims just as a badge of general belongingness, and this was a central point for Mahmut II. He was going to make an appeal to Europe, and this meant recognizing the non-Muslims as equal citizens. The prelude was important: a treaty, signed in 1838 at Balta Limanı, some way up the Bosphorus on the European side, provided for free trade with Great Britain, and British trade then boomed.

There is an important story behind this. The British had themselves followed the doctrines of Adam Smith, and were abandoning any scheme for protecting any aspect of their own economy against foreign competition, on the grounds that such protectionism would only make for laziness and parasitism. They were not far from abolishing even their protection for farmers – the Corn Laws – on the grounds that the working classes should have cheap food even if that food was not 'national'. Now, for an economy like Turkey's (the empire was so enormous that it is difficult to speak of 'an' economy at all) with only local industries, and mainly undeveloped agriculture, free trade would mean, initially, destruction: English cloth, machine-made, would sweep the board, and it did. The *stamboulines* were certainly all made from it, no doubt by very proficient tailors. Perhaps, as later nationalist commentators said, the Turks should have resisted. But Mahmut II did not have much choice.

The foreigners already had special privileges, the Capitulations, and these went back a long way, back to Süleyman the Magnificent's time, when French merchants were given certain rights; they even had Byzantine origins, in that the Venetians had exacted privileges such as relative exemption from tariffs. These were in their way quite logical. The Ottoman Empire necessarily followed the religious law, the sharia, allegedly God's own law, as revealed in the Koran and interpreted by the *ulema* to fit modern times, as and when. That law, as regards family and property, certainly did not square with European law, and one of its prescriptions, the prohibition of usury – meaning, the charging of interest on a loan – would have put banks out of business. Through the Capitulations, the European Powers were allowed their own courts (there is even a preserved British prison in the Galata district of Istanbul) and post offices. In the end, this was a sensible extension of the *millet* system by which non-Muslims could use their own private law, but of course it could be abused, as Ottoman subjects claimed foreign citizenship and thence protection by the embassies on the other side of the Horn. At any rate, there was no way in which the Ottoman government could manage its own economy along protectionist lines, and Mahmut II went in quite the opposite direction, expecting that free trade would bring in British capital, as indeed it did. Following the Treaty of Balta Limanı, the Turks started to get a good press in Britain, and as young, well-mannered, rather exotic Turks, speaking good English or French, now appeared, there was quite a vogue for the country.

In 1839 the Turks went a step further. The new sultan, Abdülmecit I, gathered the foreign diplomats together for a formal meeting at the Rose Pavilion (Gülhane) in the gardens of the Topkapı Palace, and there, his grand vizier, the formidable Mustafa Reşit Pasha, one-time ambassador in London, read out a long, involved document, couched in cumbersome religious language. Some of the diplomats did not even take the point that this was a revolutionary moment. But it was. It said that the empire had gone through disasters, that all good Muslims must recognize that they were being punished for not heeding Holy Writ, that the time had come for the old wisdoms to be restated. These were then restated, to the effect that all subjects of the Sultan should be equal before the law – meaning that Christians and Jews should cease to be second-class citizens. This was the prelude to a whole set of reforms, known, overall, as the *Tanzimat*, an Arabic plural meaning 'house in order'. There would be a modern currency (it worked, after a bad start with paper) and a centralized administration; there would be a proper law code; religion would be confined to a proper place, whatever that was supposed to be; the Turkish Empire, as foreigners called it, would be 'modernized', and part of this would mean allowing Christians to improve their lot, with schools and churches. Egypt had already moved in this direction, and Tunisia was not far behind, but even so, for an empire as large and varied as the Ottoman, this was a tremendous step.

Abdülmecit scored other points. Himself quite a good chocolate-box figure in the approved Prince Albert portrait style, he gained plaudits from the West because of a particularly generous action. In 1848, there had been revolutions all over continental Europe and the liberals, much-loved in England, had generally lost. Hungarians and Poles, who had fought reactionary Austria and Russia and lost, fled to Turkey. The Austrians wanted them to be extradited. The Sultan refused, and many of them went on to serve him in various ways – in some cases, even becoming ancestors of dynasties that made professional running in all sorts of ways in Republican Turkey (including managing the radio, introducing piano teaching, spear-heading the Communist Party and now running banks).

In this period, there occurred the first moment at which Turkey could be considered among the progressive Powers: the Crimean War. It broke out with a Russo-Turkish war in 1853, the British and French (and later the Italians) joining Turkey in 1854. It was first fought in the southern Balkans and then, when the Russians had pulled out of there, in the Crimean peninsula in the Black Sea. The causes of this war seem surreal: they lay ostensibly in Jerusalem, and concerned the guardianship of the Holy Places of Christianity – the church of the Holy Sepulchre, built by the Crusaders, and that of the Holy Nativity in Bethlehem. The Orthodox were predominant, and were supported by Russia, but the French pushed the Catholic cause, and the monks – sometimes literally, and to the merriment of the Turks – fought (as they sometimes still do: in the Holy Sepulchre, there has to be a very strict timetable as to which set of Christians does what, when). In France there was a restless, ambitious new ruler, Napoleon's nephew. He was relying on the Church to keep the peasants in line on his side, and also meant to take revenge for the defeat of 1812 and the retreat from Moscow. So he provoked trouble – demanding from the Sultan the right to protect the Holy Places, a demand delivered at Constantinople by, of all people, Baudelaire's unloved stepfather. The Tsar was angry, and sent another bully with another set of demands.

It was around this time that Tsar Nicholas I delivered himself of a famous phrase. He talked to the British ambassador and said, more or less, that Turkey was 'the sick man of Europe'. He implied that Britain and Russia could just partition the empire between them, excluding, therefore, France. But the British did not want Russians sailing warships from the Black Sea into the eastern Mediterranean, threatening British communications with India, 'the jewel in the crown', from which much of their prosperity came. There was really much more than that to this war. Russia, in 1850, counted as the great bad state, an evil empire, offering at home feudalism and tyranny, and, abroad, oppression of assorted liberal heroes. This was an ideological war, and since the Balta Limanı treaty for free trade, and the declaration of the Rose Garden for reforms, the Turks counted as progressive. The *Tanzimat* men guessed that now was their moment. If they provoked the Russians, then the Russians would maybe make a mistake, and that duly happened: Turkish and Russian troops clashed on the lower Danube and this time the Turks gave quite a good account of themselves, as the New Army entered the field. The British navy arrived in the Bosphorus, with a French cohort. Then, in November 1853, the Russians made another mistake, raiding the harbour at Sinop in the middle of the Turkish Black Sea coast. A Turkish supply fleet was smashed, by surprise, and so was much of the town, one of the oldest and most picturesque places on that coast. This caused a British response and in March 1854 Britain and France declared war on Russia.

The Crimean War was the first modern war. In the first place, there was an electric telegraph to report events within the day, and that reached the Crimea itself by 1855. Tsar Nicholas I himself learned in St Petersburg what was happening from the London *Times*. Newspapers became involved, and therefore, also, public opinion: for that reason, Florence Nightingale managed to defeat the brutal old army doctors who were running the hospital at the Selimiye Barracks in Üsküdar (Scutari), and an appalled public subscribed enormous sums to her fund. (The ambassador loathed her, and had an ingenious revenge. He got Queen Victoria to write to the Sultan proposing, as a memorial to the Crimean dead, the first Christian church built in the city since 1453. It is quite a good example of Victorian gothic, put up by G. E. Street, architect of the Law Courts on the Strand, whose pupil had been William Morris. That satisfactorily diverted money from Florence Nightingale's funds.)[1] That photographs could now be printed efficiently meant that the public could visualize what was happening. Then again, there was the first modern rifle – the Minié, longer in range than anything available to the Russians. Finally, there was the steam engine, which enabled troops to proceed more or less predictably in a week's voyage from Marseilles to the Dardanelles, whereas earlier that journey, by sail, could amount to a storm-tossed month. The British and French could manage these things and won such battles as they chose to fight in the Crimea; in 1855 after an epic, they managed to take their objective, the naval base and fortress of Sevastopol. In 1856, the Russians, their finances in a mess, their Tsar dead – Nicholas I invited death, taking a parade in the snow when he already had a bad cold – and the new Tsar keen to reform everything, made peace in 1856. There followed twenty years of peace, as far as Turkey was concerned.

How did she use it? This is the period of 'the second *Tanzimat*', associated with the successor of Abdülmecit, Abdülaziz (r. 1861–76). It started off with a restatement of the legal equality promises of 1839, and from now on the non-Muslims did indeed flourish. They grew in number faster than the Muslims, whose birth rates stagnated, prospered financially and, in particular, had increased educational opportunities. American missionaries set up schools, always with a practical, vocational side. In the 1860s, laws came thick and fast to guarantee property, to encourage banks, to underpin foreign investment, and this flowed, especially as regards railways. Soon, the

1 The Crimean Memorial Church (Christ Church) was rescued after 1991 by a very enterprising clergyman, Canon Ian Sherwood, who defied a challenge by his superiors to have the place deconsecrated. Raising support from British and American business, he restored the church, using the crypt to house refugees, for whose children he organized voluntary schooling. The church is generally about two-thirds full, and on the great occasions full to overflowing.

European parts of Constantinople, Salonica and Smyrna were integrated into the European network, and railways from them, snaking into the interior, lifted off parts of Thrace or western Anatolia, even as far as Cappadocia, to the east of Ankara. In 1861, (mainly) foreigners clubbed together and set up the Ottoman Bank, with palace-like headquarters in Galata, in what became known as 'Bank Street'.

Be it said that, in this, Turkey was far from being unique. The 1860s are a curious period, what might be called 'the first End of History'. In the early 1990s, after the Soviet Union collapsed, an American sage, Francis Fukuyama, pronounced that that was that as far as headline history was concerned: the world would just turn into a huge Denmark, as democracy and the free market spread their magic. For several years, Russians (and Chinese) perhaps believed this, and the world moved in that direction. In the 1860s, the enormous success of British ways had worldwide effect: a constitution, elections, proper laws, a national bank, a decent budget, stable money based on the Gold Standard. One Italian prime minister dyed his beard white so as to obtain English authority. Everywhere, too, there was belief in education, so schools and even universities started up, often with imposing buildings. In Russia, such were the reforms of Alexander II, but they had their counterpart in Turkey. The second *Tanzimat* was such a time.

It was symbolized by the establishment of two grand schools. Americans founded Robert College, where the teaching was in English, and it eventually acquired a fabulous site overlooking the Bosphorus (now occupied by Boğaziçi University, as the present school has buildings elsewhere). In 1868, the Sultan opened his own, Galatasaray Lycée, right in the centre of the European quarter, the (foreign-owned) trams shuttling up and down the Grande Rue de Pera past the vast iron gates of the ochre-coloured academy, attended, half and half, by Muslims and non-Muslims, with a French headmaster and a largely foreign staff. Another headmaster, ten years later, oddly enough attempted a *coup d'état*, which had something of a religious inspiration though he himself (Ali Suavi) was a very learned man with an English wife. And that was characteristic, for the second *Tanzimat* was breeding up a poison that was to kill it – exactly as Alexander II had done, with his unwitting encouragement of terrorism. The problem with this sort of enlightenment was that it could end in tears – as Fyodor Dostoyevsky extraordinarily foresaw when he wrote *Demons* in 1871. The intelligentsia might turn to terror: in 1881 Alexander II was assassinated. Abdülaziz himself had died in mysterious circumstances five years before, dethroned and probably murdered.

An enormous problem for these rulers was straightforward: money. In the Turkish case, the problem was made worse because of competition with the rulers of Egypt, who were throwing money all around the Bosphorus (the buildings sometimes survive) because they had the revenues of the new Suez Canal. The Ottoman family and its hangers-on also spent. The Dolmabahçe Palace had already been put up on the European side of the Bosphorus, a very lavish affair, with a huge chandelier, presented by Queen Victoria, and other exceptionally ugly artefacts (the paintings, sub-academy, are particularly depressing). Then came the Beylerbeyi Palace, on the Asiatic side, which, thanks to its Armenian architect, was quite comfortably proportioned and liveable-in (one of its first guests was the French empress Eugénie). It was followed by the Çırağan Palace; not so bad. But otherwise the dynasty spent and spent, its finances dependent on Armenian bankers in Galata and foreign lenders, who managed to get very favourable terms. This period of easy optimism – Sultan Abdülaziz visiting the West, his nephew Murat charming Paris, an ingenious concert of Turkish music performed for Queen Victoria in the Crystal Palace – came to an end in the early 1870s. There was a financial crash in Vienna, which spread through Germany, and the loans ceased to flow in Constantinople. In 1875 bankruptcy was declared. The empire had moved into the final act.

142.
Le Pont de Galata.

SEVEN End of Empire

Almost a century to the day after the Treaty of Küçük Kaynarca, the empire faced another great disaster. The bankruptcy of 1875 alienated British and French bond-holders, though in truth they had driven too hard a bargain, and the empire had paid back the debt several times over in interest, without paying ('amortizing') the principal. But there was worse. To pay for this ratchet, taxes went up, and the Christians had started a rebellion. It went back to Ottoman Crete, where Greek nationalists agitated for union with Greece, although a good third of the population was Muslim, and they rose in 1866, with much massacre. Then in 1875 the peasants of Herzegovina rebelled against taxes – or at any rate against attempts to put down the smuggling of tobacco, the stock-in-trade of those parts. That rebellion spread across the border to Serbia, and it in turn spread into the lands of the Bulgarians. Here there were complications. Medieval Bulgaria had had a Balkan empire, stretching into Greece and towards the Adriatic, but it had collapsed before the Turks, who had in effect run the place through Greeks, who dominated the Church. American missionaries had arrived, and they did something to standardize or even invent the language and make people literate in it; before then, respectable Bulgarians spoke Greek. What was the relationship of Bulgarian to Church Slavonic? Bulgarian nationalism was a strange product, but it emerged.

However, the Bulgarian lands had also had to receive refugees from the earlier Russian wars, and there were Tatars and Circassians all around, joining the Muslims – Pomaks – who had lived there for centuries and on the whole had decent relations with their Christian neighbours. In the second *Tanzimat*, an energetic governor, Midhat Pasha, had done quite well in building up town services, but relations between the Circassian refugees and the Bulgarian locals were tense, as they were in eastern Anatolia with the Armenians. At the first hint of trouble, there were massacres of Christians by Circassians, who feared that yet again they were going to be driven into exile. News came through to Britain that 'horrors' were happening. It was the massacre of Chios all over again.

The Liberals were by nature divided, as the Irish Question was to show, but they could be united by an astute leader on a single issue. There was one very solid element among them, Protestant Dissenters who did not subscribe to the official Church of England. These were precisely the sort of people who would get very worked up indeed at the stories of oriental cruelty against Christians, and and the great Liberal leader William Ewart Gladstone launched into tirades against the Turks. He stumped the country, and his peroration went into history: the Turks should get out, bag and baggage, zaptiehs (*zaptiyes*) and mudirs, from the provinces that they had desolated and profaned. What was so odd about this was that Gladstone knew the Balkans directly, because he had, in an 'out' period, been governor of the Ionian Isles, which the British had occupied in 1815. He knew that the problems were not so simple. Besides, when it came to massacres, the Bulgarians were no innocents – a fact that was quite easily identified by the British embassy in Constantinople, which had its agents on the ground. The ambassador, Austen Henry Layard, even protested to the foreign secretary, Lord Salisbury, that Gladstone was lying. This did not make any difference.

A curious collection of would-be high-minded clergymen, professors of English history who did not know anything substantial about the area, seem to have acquired a caricature vision of the Turks, lolling around in harems, smoking hashish and ravishing virgins. As A. J. P. Taylor pointed out, these people had had a very good chance to make a public protest about a matter in their own purlieu. In Jamaica, not long before, a Governor Eyre had broken the law in order to hang 'negro' rebels; there had been an outcry from people who had taken up the anti-slavery cause; and the Bulgarian-horrors people, including Gladstone, had either been silent, or had supported Governor Eyre. He had been condemned by a roll call (minus Thomas Carlyle) of all that was best in that period: John Stuart Mill, Charles Darwin, Thomas Huxley. The Bulgarian team was the second eleven. Gladstone himself was a wonderful moralizer, but his diaries, written in Greek, record the masturbation fantasies that he could control, even when chancellor of the exchequer, only by applying a little golden whip to himself. And did that phalanx of indignant Dissenters somehow sense that, within a decade or two, their churches would be emptying if they did not find some new cause? Whatever: the Turks were again driven onto the defensive, able only to bluster in reply, as ever, that nothing was wrong, that the numbers were exaggerated and that anyway it had been the victims' just deserts.

In 1876 the Russians sensed that, now, they had a chance to undo the verdict of the Crimean War. This time, the British would not interfere – even Lord Salisbury, for the Conservatives, was writing off Turkey, and looking to partnership with Russia. True, the Austrians were at that time strong in the Near East, and would naturally resent any Russian monopoly. But they too could be squared with promises of land in the western Balkans, and the offer of a profitable railway to Salonica. In the middle of all of this, Abdülaziz was overthrown. His successor, young Murat V (r. 1876), was paraded as a liberal sovereign, and one of the brightest men in modern Turkish history, Midhat Pasha, argued for a proper constitution. This was really a way of silencing western opposition, and was even announced in dramatic circumstances, at a conference of the Powers at the Porte. How could the Powers interfere in Ottoman affairs, if the empire had been turned overnight into a constitutional and parliamentary state? An election and a parliament did indeed make their appearance. There was, of course, much more to this than met the eye, and Midhat had to argue his way through formidable opposition, on occasion getting his allies to argue that 'consultation is needed' was found in the Koran – true, but in the context of what a divorcing man could say to his wife about breast-feeding. He himself was possibly a republican, but in the first place, elections would mean Muslim majorities, and that attracted the religious conservatives: they would have their Islamic state, and not the godless *Tanzimat* arrangements. But in any case the Powers withdrew their ambassadors, in protest at what they saw as a manoeuvre by which the Turks could put off further intervention by the Powers, and the Russian army crossed the Danube.

The Russian idea was to advance in a pincer attack, the eastern arm concentrated in the southern Caucasus to take the great fortress of Kars and to establish a presence in eastern Anatolia. Here was ancient Armenia; already, the province of Yerevan (roughly, today's Armenia) was being set up by the Russians as a Christian outpost, many of its Muslim (mainly Kurdish and Azeri, Persianized Turks) inhabitants being cleared out. But in the Balkans was another possible Russian satellite: Bulgaria. After the Balkan rebellion of 1875, the Powers had tried to force the Turks to recognize at least a semi-independent Bulgaria and when this was refused the Russians declared war. They began well, and then tried to cross the Balkan mountains, via the fortress of Plevna. And here, in the winter of 1877–78, they ran into one of the Turkish verities: that when attacked, Turkish soldiers would show extraordinary fortitude. Osman Pasha became the hero of the hour, resisting Russian attacks for months on end, and this was enough to tip the balance of public opinion in Britain. There, wise men considered that the essential was to defend India against Russian encroachments, and the defence would begin at Constantinople. The navy was sent to Besika Bay, just south of Troy, where there was an anchorage relatively safe from autumn storms. Later, the ships – 'Ironclads' – steamed into the Sea of Marmara. In any case the Ottoman navy was being trained by British officers, under Hobart Pasha, who was a popular figure. Everything was set for a great clash and perhaps on Crimean lines.

As matters turned out, Osman Pasha did in the end surrender, and Russian troops got as far as a place then known as San Stefano, now Yeşilköy in the western suburbs of Istanbul, and the site of today's Atatürk airport. An armistice was declared and then a treaty imposed: at Russian dictation, an independent Greater Bulgaria was set up, and the Russians acquired north-eastern Anatolia, including Kars, with a substantial Armenian population. Then the other Powers, led by the British, protested. The Germans offered to mediate and in 1878 held an international conference in Berlin (to which the Turks were almost not invited at all). In the upshot, the Treaty of Berlin created a lesser Bulgaria ruled by a German prince (Alexander of Battenberg, great uncle of the Duke of Edinburgh), though theoretically still under the Sultan, and a Bulgarian province of the empire, Eastern Rumelia, under a Christian governor. In 1885 the province was fused with the Bulgarian principality by a bloodless coup.

And now a fateful step occurred. The Armenians, so far, had not made trouble – quite the contrary, they co-operated very well with the Turks, not least because their real rivals were the Greeks and the Jews. Now, their Patriarch talked to the Russians, and tried for a place at the Berlin Congress. He did not get very far: the Russians themselves did not much care for Armenian nationalists, regarding them as potentially revolutionary and anyway likely to side with the West. The Russian viceroy of the Caucasus in Tiflis (modern Tbilisi) in Georgia closed down the Armenian church, on the grounds that weapons were hidden by it. But the Powers at the very least declared that they would take an official interest in the Armenians of the Ottoman Empire. That question had been 'internationalized'.

There had been some earlier internationalization. The Lebanon, part of Ottoman Syria, had a mixed population, with Christians (Maronites) and Muslims of different sorts, including the heretical Druzes. Once the *Tanzimat* had proclaimed equality, the Christians, with French support, got ahead as regards schooling and commerce; there was rioting in Damascus; French troops landed in Beirut, then a growing port; the Ottoman commissioner, Fuat Pasha, bloodily restored order; and in 1860 Lebanon acquired a special status, with a Christian governor and power-sharing arrangements, which the French in particular had a right to supervise. This was the first real piece of internationalization, and it appeared to work well for several generations. Lebanon did not blow up again until 1960, even then on a small scale (at least in comparison with the horrors to come in the 1970s). The question to be asked as to such internationalization is: would the various elements have come to an understanding among themselves, if they had not been able to throw responsibility on some outside authority? At any rate, here, along with Bulgaria, was a precedent for 'Armenia', and among the Armenians, nationalism grew. In the 1860s the ecclesiastics who had dominated their affairs hitherto were displaced, in favour of merchants and professional men who greatly promoted schools.

Then in the 1880s, whether in Tiflis – at that stage, the town with the largest Armenian population – or abroad, in Switzerland, revolutionary parties grew up. They had learned their stuff in Russia, and even took Russian names – one of them from *Bell* ('Hintchak' in Armenian), the title of the best-known revolutionary periodical. That stuff included terror. Assassinate a Tsar, provoke the police; the police will be stupid and heavy-handed; they will beat up innocents; the innocents' families will then sympathize with the terrorists. The Armenian nationalists ended up in the Russian parliament as the Bolsheviks' only allies. That young Armenians clustered in American mission schools also mattered, as they became deluded, to the effect that the Christian West would come to their help.

Meanwhile, in eastern Anatolia, tensions rose. The Circassians had been expelled (maybe one and a half million, including Chechens) from the Caucasus by the Russians and, having lost a third of their people in overcrowded boats and otherwise gruesome circumstances, had gathered there, and fought over land with the local Armenians; the same happened with nomadic Kurds, who descended in the winter on Armenian villages and expected to be fed and housed. The local officials took bribes for protection and otherwise for tax reductions. By the later 1880s, here and there, fighting started.

Murat V had reigned well meaningly over affairs. However, he lasted only for a few months in 1876, and was pushed out ostensibly on grounds of mental feebleness (he understandably found everything a strain) and was succeeded by a far abler younger brother, Abdülhamit II, who managed to stay on the throne until 1909. Poor Murat had behaved quite loyally towards Midhat Pasha, who had made the constitution. Abdülhamit played a longer and more astute game, co-operating with Midhat to gain the confidence, especially of the British, and then disposing of him to long years of exile and eventually murder, in Saudi Arabia. The fact was that Abdülhamit did not believe in liberalism and constitutions; they would only divide the empire. Tsar Alexander II and still more his son Alexander III thought much the same, and relations with Russia became surprisingly warm: the fact was that the two empires had a great deal in common. Now, after the Treaty of Berlin, the Turkish one was becoming much more pronouncedly Muslim. The Bulgarians, in effect, had their own national Christian state; so did the Greeks and the Serbs, and Muslims fled in droves as ethnic cleansing happened and mosques were knocked down. The Austrians had occupied Bosnia, the British, Cyprus: more refugees. In 1881 the Greek boundary was extended to the north, with British encouragement, and the Ottoman presence in the southern Balkans was now confined to Albania and Macedonia. There were of course millions of Christians and Jews still in the empire, but they were now in a minority – under one-fifth.

Abdülhamit meant to give unity to an empire that consisted of various Muslims, essentially Turks and Arabs. His predecessors had preached the gospel of Ottomanism from the European-style Dolmabahçe Palace. Abdülhamit retired to the more secluded Yıldız, just up the hill from it, and made much more of the Islamic aspects of the empire. It was now that a myth was developed, that the Ottomans had all along been wagers of Holy War, and the tombs of the early Sultans at Bursa were given the standard late-nineteenth-century historical-triumphalist treatment with such a claim in mind. Abdülhamit also disbanded the parliament and ruled by decree; he soon acquired a ferocious reputation abroad – *le saigneur*, ran Anatole France's pun, referring to the blood that this Sultan *seigneur* was supposed to have shed; 'Abdul the Damned', as the would-be Gladstones called him. There was certainly a larger police network than before, and one Arap İzzet Pasha busied himself at Ramazan, ferociously punishing anyone caught eating or smoking near the Yıldız Palace. But Abdülhamit was a considerable figure: a very skilled carpenter, and even a translator of opera. His energy was remarkable (he regarded himself as being above Koranic rules, and took seven wives, the last married in 1900, when she was seventeen and he fifty-eight). He turned his back on the *Tanzimat* bureaucrats, especially Midhat Pasha.

Certainly, the emphasis was on religion, and at that sometimes in utterly obscurantist form. Ordinary people did not have a chance of understanding the Koran, and an enterprising Turk translated it from the classical Arabic. The translation was banned. Much the same happened with insurance. That counted as blasphemy, because why? God willed that your house was burned down, and it did not do to seek compensation. When the constitution was discussed, the arguments were in religious language. Cabinets seriously talked (or, more likely, pretended to) talk this nonsense, but Abdülhamit obviously reckoned that a strengthened Islam would keep his empire together, would bind Arabs and Turks. It all strangely foreshadows the Turkey to come, where an Islamic-Turkish synthesis is always on the stove and somehow never seems to come to the boil: as had been the case since Selim III, the army was the truly creative force.

On the other hand, Abdülhamit did a great deal for education, even introducing girls' schools, and he encouraged the Christian element of the population: there were Armenians in high places all over, and his bankers were Greek. The Christian schools flourished, Robert College especially, along with the French and other European establishments, but also the

Greek and Armenian ones. Abdülhamit also built up technical institutions, schools of engineering, medicine, and even business (at that, on the very Hippodrome next to the Blue Mosque to give it prestige) and encouraged the modernization of Islam. At the time, there were rabid conservatives who regarded the West and all its works as damned. If they were told that the medicine and science were just far better, the answer would come back that it was Arabs, long before, who had invented such improvements.

It took an Abdülhamit to push through the changes, and he crowned them by building what was shown off as the first Muslim-built railway, designed to take pilgrims to Mecca (and, less poetically, to shift troops to hold the Saudi and Yemeni populations down, and especially the Beduin who raided the pious columns). This Sultan even managed to take hold of finances. He was himself very mean, but he was also an entrepreneur on his own behalf, developing marshlands in Iraq, for instance. But the chief aspect of this was his co-operation with the foreign bond-holders. In 1881 they had come to an agreement, on much the same lines as occurred in Egypt and, for that matter, Greece. A Caisse de la Dette Publique Ottomane was set up in 1881, and it soon acquired a very fine building, designed by the Levantine Alexandre Vallaury, with extraordinary gabling, next to the Persian embassy in Cağaloğlu (it is now the Istanbul Boys' School). A staff of 5,000 collected certain earmarked taxes to pay the bond-holders, getting them to accept less usurious profits; and the building itself, which dominated its section of the Horn (and which is now illuminated at night) was a standing reminder to the population that western capitalism had the country in its grip. There was a similar effect on the European side, for the Sultan, because if he looked to the north-west, up the hill towards Pera, he would see, first, the German embassy, with four gigantic bronze eagles on the roof (it was known as 'the bird cage', and someone – how? – managed to winch the eagles down from the roof one night in 1919; they have never been seen again) and then the Russian one, the vice-royalty to end all vice-royalties.

In practice, the Ottoman Debt Office did some good. Interest rates, though at 7 per cent high, had fallen and considerable foreign investment did come in; the Debt Office was trusted and it gave good advice. Foreign banks arrived, building the elaborate late-Victorian palaces now to be seen just over the Galata Bridge (the present-day structure's predecessor, now moored some way up the Horn, being a novelty of that era) and in Abdülhamit's time the infrastructure was greatly improved, with railways and trams, though not, on the whole, roads that were better than tracks. Salonica, Smyrna, Constantinople and Adana did quite well and sometimes splendidly, but so also did provincial places such as Bursa or Ankara, which acquired some decent government buildings once the railway came (1892). They had good governors – in the case of Bursa, Ahmet Vefik Bey, who translated Molière, put up a library and a theatre, and, with broad streets setting off the great monuments, established that town as one of the most prosperous and best-ordered in today's Turkey; Abidin Pasha managed something of the same feat in old Ankara.

Constantinople had acquired a town-plan in the early *Tanzimat* era, and at least the European quarter had been modernized (although the targeted ratepayers at the start torpedoed the project, and had to be forced in the end to accept proper sewage arrangements and gas lighting). These things involved a flouting of the sharia law, but in the end the many great fires caused by the close juxtaposition of flimsy wooden structures cleared the way for proper 'urbanization': that, plus a consciousness as to how the Europeans regarded existing arrangements with contempt. There is a characteristic document of the 1860s, in which the powers-that-be speak schizophrenically: we have the most beautiful and sublime city in the world, but foreigners regard it as dreadful. By now, any thinking Muslim was bound to ask why, in the poet Ziya Pasha's words, everywhere they went the Christians had palaces and the Muslims lived in slums – an exaggeration, but fair enough. There were of course foolish reactionaries who shut their eyes and said either that it was not true or it was the will of God or that it was His punishment on Muslims for not being Islamic enough. It was such people, earlier on, who had even managed to close down the first university in Constantinople on two separate occasions. However, intelligent commentators knew that Islam was backward and they were very keen to install the wisdoms of the West as far as engineering or medicine were concerned, though of course in a religious context. Abdülhamit did remarkably well, given the background. He re-founded the university (it was called 'Imperial House of Applied Sciences') in 1900 and was careful to keep it on religious lines, the argument being that proper science had come from Islam, but that the application of it had been neglected and left to westerners. In other ways, as well, he introduced modern subjects in schools that had originally been set up for religious purposes – rote-learning of the Koran and the like, by enthusiasts who did not understand a word.

The problem here was that the Sultan was training up enemies. If bright young men (and, more and more, women) learned modern subjects and the attitudes that went with them, they were not likely to remain affectionate towards an Islamic regime that was on occasion tyrannical (in fact Abdülhamit was only occasionally tyrannical, certainly by later standards, and seldom applied the death sentence). But there were two classes of men, especially, who would turn against him. The first was medical. Medicine was a school for atheism, and a training in the natural sciences did not inspire much affection for Holy Writ that was so demonstrably wide of the mark in explaining the world. By now, many Turks were learning French, reading the philosopher Ernest Renan or (a then famous account of Islam) Reinhard Dozy; they could see for themselves how much richer and better organized were the cities of Europe.

The second class of rebels consisted of army officers, now being given a professional training. They particularly resented the low pay and the domination by duds, a weakness of the Hamidian regime being of course that the Sultan did not want clever and ambitious subordinates. He allowed the navy to rot in the Horn, though that happened in some degree because naval demonstrations at the Dolmabahçe Palace had overthrown his two predecessors. He also economized on expenses, partly because he was by nature cheeseparing and mainly because the foreigners of the Debt Office controlled affairs. The result, as the Ottoman general Sadettin Pasha moaned in 1896, when he was sent to pacify Van, then rent by a horrible Kurdish-Armenian war (the Kurds were better at it), was that his troops wore a ragbag of uniforms and the officers sold the extra allocations of rice rations to the sneering local Armenians to make up their woeful salaries.

Then again, whatever Abdülhamit could do for the towns of Anatolia, he still had to face the Balkan problem. Macedonia, with a very mixed population, was the hinterland of the great port of Salonica, and the peace could be kept only with a military effort. The Albanians, since the Berlin decisions, had been responding gingerly to notions of eventual independence, although they had so far been the most loyal element. On Crete, the peace was maintained only with difficulty, and with European participation that already revealed one of the central truths of such international involvements: that the peacekeepers did not intend to lose their own lives, would therefore find excuses to co-operate with the stronger side, would then tell lies about this (foreshadowing later events on Cyprus and in Bosnia where, it was alleged, the inhabitants of Sarajevo had been shelling themselves). The Greeks took encouragement from this, but did so after another crisis altogether had boiled over: 'the Armenian massacres' of 1894–96, which gave Gladstone an encore for his zaptiehs and mudirs, though, this time, rather ragged.

There were rival Armenian revolutionary parties, whose leaders imagined that they could provoke intervention by the western Powers, especially the British. In the later 1880s, there were flare-ups – a shot fired mysteriously at Muslims going about their business opposite the American hospital in Erzurum (missionaries were alleged to be encouraging Armenian separatism), followed by ransackings and then the putting up of shop shutters; an affray at a mountain stronghold called Zeytun, where Armenians were supposed to be hiding weapons in a church; another at Sasun, south-west of Lake Van. In 1890 all of this spread to Constantinople and in the Armenian quarter of Kumkapı on the Sea of Marmara there was a big demonstration, which got out of hand. The fact was that a significant proportion of the Armenians (and of course Muslims, who had perfectly good relations with them all along) did not want trouble. In Constantinople, numbers of them were prosperous, many others did useful jobs, and without the Armenians cultural life would have been vastly impoverished: the Théâtre des Petits Champs, built on the lesser cemetery in Pera (the meaning of *petits champs (des morts)*, now the site of the TRT television building), was an essential pioneer, soon complemented by other theatres and cinemas on the Grande Rue de Pera.

The Armenian church, especially, wished to avoid trouble. In 1894 a patriarch, Ashikyan, said as much in a sermon: the Armenians have lived with the Turks for a thousand years, have been allies from the start; have flourished; are nowhere a majority in the Ottoman Empire; if the nationalists have their way they will provoke the destruction of our people. A young nationalist then fired some shots at him. Assassinations went on and on, leading to the death in 1912 of an Armenian mayor of Van, who, again, had been desperately warning the nationalists that their enterprises would end in tears. However, the Armenians of the diaspora were astute in presenting their case to a West, and especially a Protestant and Atlantic West, that was only too willing to believe what they said. That well over a million Muslim refugees had been expelled from the Crimea or the Balkans or the Caucasus, losing perhaps a third of their numbers to depradations and disease, did not seem to count for anything, and yet it was the clash of these refugees with the Armenians of eastern Anatolia that was causing a good part of the problem.

What was Abdülhamit to do? In 1891 he played the Kurdish card. The Russians had famously recruited Cossacks (and a 'savage division' from the northern Caucasus) to preserve order in frontier areas. In eastern

Anatolia and in mountainous western Persia there were Kurdish tribes, often collected under a chieftain legendary both for ferocity and hospitality. In the name of Islamic solidarity, Abdülhamit opened what was called 'the tribal school' in Constantinople, where the sons of these chieftains could be civilized; but he also took over the horsemen of the tribes as regiments, in a force called the *Hamidiye*. In 1894 there was a particularly savage encounter between this cavalry corps and the Armenians at Sasun. The local missionaries protested, and raised the slogan of 'Armenian massacres'. Abdülhamit was accused in effect of the first 'genocide', and there were alleged to have been 300,000 Armenian deaths. A French historian, François Georgeon, joins a British colleague, Andrew Mango, in pulling the figure down to about 30,000, and further points out that, though in several of the Armenian provinces there were indeed massacres, in others (such as Muş) the governors prevented them from happening.

It was at this point that the Sultan sent Sadettin Pasha to Van to keep the peace. He addressed the Kurdish chieftains, and said there was to be no persecution of the Armenians: they were protected by Islam and in any case, given the telegraph, their woes would reach the European press in an hour. He told the Armenians that if it had not been for the Ottomans, the Armenians would have disappeared like the aboriginal inhabitants of Anatolia, the Lydians or the Phrygians, and he was quite right. But he agreed with a British consul that everyone lied. The Kurds denied that they stole the Armenians' sheep and the Armenians multiplied by five the number of sheep stolen. Still, there had been some well-documented horrors, and since 1894 international pressure (not from Germany) had grown. However, the Powers could not agree as to what might be done, and there were only stale offers of reform.

In September 1895 the Hintchaks in Constantinople had forced the pace with a demonstration, in which the police became involved; there were outrages in Harput, in eastern Anatolia, where there was a famous American college (again, the missionaries were accused of encouraging Armenian nationalism); in August 1896 came a terrorist spectacular, when members of the Armenian Dashnak party cleverly got into the Ottoman Bank in Galata, did some killing, took hostages, and threatened to blow up the entire building. That one was uneasily settled when the terrorists were escorted out of the country on the French ambassador's yacht. Following this, there was a regular flare-up of the Muslims in Constantinople against Armenians in general, and hundreds, or maybe even thousands, were killed. Then matters died down again. Armenian diaspora nationalists have never forgiven the British for what they see as a betrayal, but Lord Salisbury pointed out that, whatever else the Royal Navy could do, it could not sail up Mount Ararat. Only the Russians could re-create Armenia. Far from wishing to do so, their Caucasus viceroy regarded Armenians as revolutionaries, and when the Armenian disaster finally happened, in 1915, the deputy viceroy of the Caucasus remarked that the Turks had given them what they wanted, an Armenia without Armenians.

The British had nevertheless turned against Turkey, and Salisbury had really written her off. They had another possible ally, or even satellite: Greece. It is an odd fact that, right up to 1947, the British were so closely involved, to the point of intervening in her civil wars, even though, with India and Palestine, their own plate was more than full, and the dollars were running out (in the end, the British threw the problem at Washington). The Greeks were good at playing London, certainly much better than the Turks: they had a – the – Indo-European language, had shipping money, masonic connections and, with marriages often enough in surprisingly high places, the right invitations. They were especially good at cultivating the Liberal Party.

Crete, so mountainous as to be impossible for the Ottomans to control, was in ferment, and the nationalist leader, Eleftherios Venizelos, had charisma. There *were* Muslims on Crete, roughly one third of the population. Cretan nationalists simply said that their ancestors had been forced or bribed to convert, that the Christians were anyway much more go-ahead, and that re-conversion would be an act of charity. Liberals agreed: 'the Turk' meant indolence, erotic stupour, epidemics and oppression. This was

Gladstone, with a reedy and none too convincing tone, but the Greeks provoked trouble, in the expectation that the British would come to their rescue. In 1897 there was a brief war, which the Turks won. But the Greek expectation was not wrong because the British forced Abdülhamit not to take advantage of the victory. Within a decade, Crete was in effect free, and what the world now knows as 'ethnic cleansing' went ahead – the Muslims cruelly pushed out, with a great deal of killing. If, two generations later, the Turks resisted very strongly over Cyprus, where there was a comparable situation, this needs to be put in context.

By 1900, the Hamidian regime – it used to be known in Turkey as 'the time of tyranny', but in the past decade there has been considerable rethinking – was unravelling. The humiliations at the hands of foreigners were causing huge resentments, and there was one up-and-coming case that provided a focus. Macedonia straddled four of today's Balkan countries, each with its ambitions. Greeks saw themselves as the civilizing element – Alexander the Great. Serbians thought that the port of Salonica would turn them into a proper European state. Bulgarians could claim that the Slav Macedonians were really Bulgars (arguments about the language go back and forth). There were as well Albanians, whose national consciousness was slowly asserting itself. The area had also fallen into banditry, and an Ottoman army, based on Salonica, had its work cut out to control affairs. In 1903 the Powers, for separate reasons, agreed not to fight over the area. Austria and Russia, especially, took a lead, and proposed a degree of internationalization: there would be a foreign police force, with neutral Dutchmen to run it. Order was not restored, and the presence of foreigners only excited the various nationalists to write off the Turks altogether. There was even a fear that the Arabs, supposedly the master race of the Islamic world, were dropping out as Arab separatism grew. In June 1908, as part of another shift in international affairs, Tsar Nicholas II met Edward VII on the Royal Yacht at Reval (Tallinn) in the Baltic. Russia and Britain, in common apprehension at Germany's expansion, were coming at last to an agreement, an agreement such as Salisbury had imagined. Was this to amount to partition of the Ottoman Empire – the Straits for Russia, Syria for France, Egypt and the oil of Iraq for Britain?

Officers of the Third Army based in Macedonia talked, and established secret societies which, quite soon, excited mutiny. That coincided with angry talk in other places. There were, first of all, the various schools that Abdülhamit himself had set up, where young men (and even young women) had been educated on western lines. The idea had been to show that Islam could manage such techniques, including French, as well as Christianity – there is similar thinking, this time as regards computing, in the political-religious elements in the Turkish government today – and this was not unsuccessful. However, introduction to the techniques also meant some questioning; and Abdülhamit's graduates were disaffected – apart from anything else, they only needed to look out of the window to see grand foreigners and Levantines betaking themselves to the elaborate hotels, the Pera Palace or the Tokatlian, or the enormous Grand Cercle d'Orient, where ambassadors and directors of the Ottoman Debt joshed with local Greek grandees, all under the protection of the Hamidian police and its informers. Even at the grandest of the institutions, the Galatasaray Lycée, the boys could be got only with great difficulty to shout 'Long Live the Padishah'.

The system did have its defenders, there being religious reactionaries around who asserted that there was nothing wrong and anyway it was all God's will. Abdülhamit was a great deal more intelligent than this, but he himself was becoming old and tired. One sign of disintegration was that the Zionists took an interest in Palestine. Theodor Herzl came to see the Sultan, and wondered, very delicately (he was yet another Hungarian in Constantinople) whether perhaps in return for settlement of debts, Jewish immigration might go ahead in Palestine (the answer was an equally polite 'no'). In 1905 Armenians planted a bomb outside the Yıldız Mosque, timed to explode as the Sultan left. He was detained for a short talk with the Sheikh ul-Islam, and the bomb exploded, instead, in a crowd, killing or maiming some seventy people. There is a photograph of the Sultan, looking old, weary, and with the otherwise considerably dignified charm switched off: it is used quite absurdly to illustrate works of Armenian propaganda.

Then in 1908 all of the problems came to a head. In the first place, there were widespread revolts against the excessive taxation – at any rate, excessive as the era held such things – and in Erzurum Armenians and Muslims made common cause against the corrupt establishment of a governor. That revolt spread, and was contained only with difficulty, sometimes with the replacement of an unpopular governor. Then came a military mutiny, in the area of the Third Army in the southern Balkans. Almost overnight, the Hamidian regime collapsed, and in July, with vast demonstrations in the centre of Constantinople, the constitution was again proclaimed. Abdülhamit was still on the throne, but as a constitutional sovereign, with a parliament to take over much of his earlier power. The men taking over from him were generally called the 'Young Turks', and in Europe there was some relief at what was called the Turkish revolution: Abdülhamit was by now a much-hated man.

'Young Turks' will have to do as shorthand, but they did not use the term themselves, and in any case they came from different quarters. Fifty years before there had been constitutional liberals who referred to themselves as 'Young Ottomans'. Mainly, they lived in exile, and their chief objection was to the secularizing *Tanzimat* state: why not return to the virtues of political Islam, under which, of course, the rights of Christians would be respected, but without the privileges that Christians were now acquiring. A parliament, representing the Muslim majority, would deal with that. In effect Abdülhamit had made such a parliament unnecessary. In 1889, on the anniversary of the French Revolution (there were cheap train tickets to, and local transport in, Paris: the Italian socialists also took advantage of this to form a party) a well-connected exile, Ahmet Rıza, collected a few dozen sympathizers and proclaimed a new party, which was eventually called the Committee of Union and Progress. Armenians joined in; so did a dissident

Ottoman prince, Sabaheddin, the Sultan's nephew. Again, the idea was Ottoman, in the sense that these men could see no alternative to co-operation between Muslims and others, but they regarded the Muslim majority as deserving a senior role, and some of them were now taking an interest in Turkishness.

Until now, the word 'Turk' was used only by foreigners, the medieval Italians having taken over *Turchia* from the Arabs. In the Ottoman Empire, there were jokes about 'crude Turks' and the court sniggered, punningly, *Etrak-i bi-idrak*, meaning 'the Turks are jerks'. The peasants spoke and recited Turkish, but although its grammar shaped Ottoman, the vocabulary of that was Arabic or Persian, on top of which the men who ran the governing institution changed the script and the vocabulary more or less as a way to keep out competition. Ottoman Turkish in the later nineteenth century was self-consciously archaizing, and is more difficult to read than the seventeenth-century versions. In the middle of the nineteenth century, journalism was starting to spread, and a bright spark or two remarked that, if the language were simplified, then readerships would increase and no doubt column-inches would be properly rewarded. There was already a well-established journalist, Namık Kemal, prepared to write in a simplified language, but the readership was still pitifully small, and 90 per cent of the published books were of a religious nature: the intelligentsia read French novels (and Abdülhamit not only adored Sherlock Holmes, but gave a high decoration to Conan Doyle).

The Young Turks' central organization contained different strands: Prince Sabaheddin was a liberal who believed in Ottoman amity and got both Armenian and Greek support; Ahmet Rıza insisted on the primacy of Muslims but in constitutional style; and then there were out-and-out secularists, not as yet many, who regarded the Ottoman past as so much junk. Abdullah Cevdet, a doctor of Kurdish origin who turned sociologist and became prominent in politics, wrote vociferously against the primacy of Koranic injunctions and even said that the Arabic script was utterly unsuitable for conveying Turkish noises. Arguments concerning education then followed: why were the Muslim schools so much more primitive than the Christian (or Jewish) ones? Graduates of the new foreign-language schools were inclined to agree. They emerged from Saint Benoît or Saint Joseph or even the girls' one, Notre Dame, at Pangaltı near the Military Academy, and scoffed at the Koranic learning-by-heart that went on in the Muslim schools.

Then there were the army officers. A secret society had developed among them, and especially in the Balkans, where many of them had been born. One such was Mustafa Kemal, subsequently known as Atatürk, although he shot to fame only later on. His father died early, and his mother sent him as a small boy to a religious school in Salonica, which he hated. He had strength of character enough, even early on, to make sure that she sent him to a cadet school, and there he did well: he was an outstanding soldier. There was a Major Enver (later Enver Pasha), born into an established Constantinople family, who had vision and a capacity for organization. They teamed up with a Macedonian official called Mehmet Talât. He was an official of the post office, but in those days this did not imply lowly origins: post offices were grand buildings, and their heads had to be men of probity.

Later on, when the religiously inclined greatly resented another bout of secularism, there was muttering to the effect that these members of the secret society were either Jews or crypto-Jews. This is because, in Salonica, there were many *Dönmes*, Jewish converts to Islam who had followed the Jewish kabbalist and convert Sabbatai Sevi over three centuries before. It was put about that these were not real Muslims, and it was unquestionably true that they took a lead in secularization: they had a foundation, even for girls' schooling, of their own in Salonica, called Işık (Light), which has in Istanbul today successor-schools and even a successor-university. Cavit Bey, a financial expert, was certainly one, but there were others, and an energetic publisher, Ahmet Yalman, sympathized. In time, there was to be complaint in Islamic quarters that these men made a republic, whereas the Sultanate should have been preserved, as representing the entire Muslim world. There is not much truth in this, though in a sense the Republic, like for that matter the empire, had been made in the Balkans.

In the summer of 1908, the officers' mutiny was completely successful and Abdülhamit retired to the Yıldız Palace. However, these officers had no experience of politics, and although there was soon a functioning parliament, the Palace still appointed the government. Practised old hands took over as grand viziers and there were troubles of various sorts. For the first time, there was a real strike, and it especially affected the railways. However, the Europeans did not give the Young Turks much leeway. The Austrians straightforwardly annexed Bosnia; the Bulgarians declared independence and their ruler made himself king; there was clear Russian connivance. Discontent grew. But there was also a religious reaction. One 'Blind Ali', a fanatic, was given covert encouragement from the Palace, and he raided parliament with soldiers of his own (known as 'the 31 March event' in Turkey, although the calendar was, like the Russian one, a fortnight or so in arrears) – an echo of the Janissary-*ulema* alliance. However, this time, the Young Turks could call upon a real 'New Army': it marched from Salonica and forced out Sultan Abdülhamit. Although he was succeeded, in turn, by two of his brothers, the dynasty had now itself become hardly more than an exhibit in the Topkapı museum. Meanwhile, how were the Young Turks, in 1909, to use their power?

EIGHT Crash

Some people have nationalism thrust upon them, and that is what happened when Abdülhamit fell. Modern Turkey starts from his fall in 1909. It was not, of course, that the Young Turks were agreed on a radical programme; they tried to control the grand viziers from behind the scenes, but they themselves became divided – any British commentator would at once say of 'Committee', 'Union' and 'Progress' that you could not have more than two of the three. There were Islamists in varying degrees; there were liberals; there were Turkish nationalists; there were secularists, men, usually with a medical background, who, as doctors so often do, regarded religion and the religious with mild contempt and more than mild bewilderment. Abdullah Cevdet, who was one of them, and by origin a Kurd, was outspoken: oh, to get rid of the ugly clothes, the howling, the repetitive stupidity, the preposterous assertion of moral superiority, the idiotic education given to the princes and the automatic blaming of Europe for anything that went wrong. Another Kurd, Ziya Gökalp, came round to the idea of a Turkish nation state. The sages of Europe, John Stuart Mill and Emile Durkheim, were to be read on this subject: the nation state was the building-block for progress. Mill thought backward tribes, such as Scottish Highlanders, Basques (and, he would have said, Kurds) should just go away. Marx had thought the same thing.

At the very least, peasants could not attain literacy unless the national language became the vehicle for education: otherwise Anatolian rurals would be lost, mumbling their way round Persian or Arabic. There was in fact a model to hand: Balkan nationalism, especially Greek. There was Ancient Greek and there was Church Greek, both of them far removed from the peasant world. An effort was made to modernize the language, which led to fancy inventions – *metafora esoterika* for 'domestic bus travel', or, splendidly, *efemerides* for 'newspapers'. But Greece won wars: could not Turkey make a similar effort at modernization, with a language even further removed from that of ordinary people? An old Turkish dictionary is indeed an adventure, containing words such as *iftihar*, described as 'the pride that a father feels in his son's achievements'; *adamsendecilik*, meaning 'being messed about with in a pointless way by someone in authority, to the point at which you need help,' is pure *sans paroles*. Peasants might, in this case, have a use for that. But if Turkey was to be modern, there would have to be a proper language, and the Young Turks began to impose the language on non-Turks. Arabs complained.

After 1908, when the censorship was lifted, there was an explosion of commentary and there was rancid debate. In this, one of the great weaknesses of the secularists soon emerged. They were, as a coterie, unshakably convinced of their own superiority, addicted to the sound of their own voices, and could not understand the recalcitrance of the lower orders. It was all reminiscent of the contemporaneous French Third Republic, where, in 1906, the Church was disestablished and nuns were driven out of convents at bayonet-point. Turkey would (as Abdullah Cevdet guessed) arrive at that point, or something similar, within twenty years. But a decade of nightmare came first.

When the Young Turks arrived in power, they did, on one level, not badly at all. In a continuation of Abdülhamit's activities, but with much more energy and with better personnel, they went ahead with improvements in communications, in the organization of towns, and in education, where, at last, girls' schools were properly pushed forward. They promoted football, now a national craze. Around 1900 the British had played it at Moda, on the Asiatic side of the Bosphorus. Young Turks wanted to follow, but the *ulema* did not approve, and so a Turkish team called 'Black Stockings' played in semi-disguise. The police stopped their first game. Clubs for the English, Greek and other minorities were established, the first one at Kadıköy, near Moda. It was not until the boys of the Galatasaray Lycée set up a club in 1905 that Turkish players participated in the fledgling Constantinople Football League, and under the Young Turks this process boomed (nowadays, for whatever reason, Galatasaray is the favoured team of the Istanbul Kurds). But that went together with a discovery of what Turkishness might mean, including some speculation (really owed to foreigners, especially Arminius Vámbéry and other Hungarians, but also to Russian Tatars who took refuge in Anatolia) as to the links with long-lost brothers in Central Asia.

At any rate, the Young Turks developed an organization that spread through Anatolia, where local groups represented the Committee of Union and Progress (CUP) – in Ankara, for instance, they acquired a stylish headquarters that subsequently housed the National Assembly. In such precincts, in much of the country, the principles of modernization were discussed, but so also were appointments and contracts: the Committee men were sure of one thing, that a 'national bourgeoisie' would have to be created, to compete with the non-Muslims, and this would mean the awarding of public contracts to them. There was also much discussion of language reform, including a change of the script. On these levels, it was a very creative period.

However, on the political level, destructiveness and confusion occurred. The parliament of 1908 had a majority of CUP sympathizers, and for a time, under a dignified and intelligent Speaker (Ahmet Rıza), it functioned with elegance and seriousness. But, as experiments in imported democracy then and later showed, the institution fatally reproduced native divisions and then made them worse – precisely as Russian reactionaries had always said would happen. The Russian Duma that emerged from the revolution of 1905 sank with all hands in June 1907, when the then prime minister pinned a notice on the door telling the deputies to go away. The Austrians got a parliament elected by universal suffrage in 1907 and it then exacerbated existing national tensions to the point at which budgets were passed by decree, deputies banged desk-lids, and the young Adolf Hitler, observing proceedings, took the point.

The Ottoman parliament, meeting in a building on the Hippodrome (it burned down and a new building went up at Fındıklı, close to the Dolmabahçe and other Bosphorus palaces), represented the empire – Christians of all sorts, Kurds, Arabs, Albanians, and so forth. You could talk whichever language you wanted (as in the Austrian parliament) and the assembly was soon at the mercy of the stupid, the self-important, the attitudinizing and the windbag. The Young Turks were anyway split, between liberals who had a sophisticated understanding of Islam and a considerable tolerance for non-Muslims, up-and-coming nationalists who had growing impatience with both of these things, and army officers who were starting to see themselves as saviours of the country.

In 1912, as foreign complications went ahead, the Young Turks even lost office. They 'fixed' an election in April 1912, but there were dissident army officers, and the opposition liberals took over, with a new party (a Greek became minister of education), in the summer. That in turn was overthrown by a coup in January 1913 when Enver Bey forced the government out at gunpoint. This was the first military coup in modern Turkish history. There were to be others, that of 1980 the most interesting. But from then on, until the last days of the First World War, the CUP was in a position to dictate. Turkish nationalism then became the order of the day. Businesses were to conduct their affairs in Turkish; the minority schools were to teach it; when war came, the hated Capitulations were abolished, and a 'national bourgeoisie' began to get the profitable contracts. This is a grubby business, leading to the confiscatory tax of 1942 and the anti-Greek pogrom of 1955. But the background matters.

An essential cause of this political turmoil was that the Turks were being thrust back to their own heartland, Anatolia. Albania and Arabs were now threatening to secede. The last year of absolute peace was 1910: the First

World War really starts with 1911 and ends in 1923, both dates having to do with Turkish affairs. In 1910–11 the Young Turks (as for short we can refer to the CUP) had a brief moment for ordinary politics, which even included a normal by-election (lost by one vote). But then the country was engulfed in war. In the summer of 1911, the French took a further step forward in Morocco, and the Germans responded with a gun-boat, the Kaiser parading himself as protector of Islam. The British publicly took the French side, and the Anglo-German rift became plain for all to see. The Italians dived into the gap and tried to seize the last Ottoman possession in North Africa – Libya; they provoked a war. On land, matters did not go well because they could seize only a narrow coastal strip and the Turks stirred up Arab tribes; however, the Italians had unquestioned superiority at sea, and used it to capture most of the southern Aegean islands, including the twelve (in fact thirteen) called the Dodecanese, Greek for 'twelve'. This in turn prompted the Balkan states: if Turkey was collapsing, then each might take its share, and there was a rare agreement between Greece, Serbia and Bulgaria over partition of the Turkish Balkans, including Albania; she, for good measure, had already a rebellion under way.

In October 1912 the Balkan states attacked. The Ottoman army was hopelessly divided, as between Anatolia, Albania, Thrace, and communications over the seas were poor. The fleet was outdone by the Greeks, who within weeks had taken Salonica, while the Bulgarians approached Constantinople itself; the Serbs took much of Macedonia and the Montenegrins invaded northern Albania. The Great Powers took alarm and insisted on an armistice, but it was broken, and the Bulgarians took Edirne. Everywhere there were Ottoman surrenders, and there were vast waves of refugees, 30,000 of them in the vicinity of the Aya Sofya itself, but spreading in hundreds of thousands all around. The horrors were well described by Leon Trotsky, as women, children and old men were driven out of villages where all the younger men had been slaughtered, gruesome priests and professors egging on the Balkan nationalists. This was the backdrop to the CUP's seizure of power in January 1913. In the event, there was a humiliating peace, in May, but the Balkan states then fought Bulgaria in a second war, which ended quickly, since the Turks intervened and recaptured Edirne – the last strip of the Ottoman Empire in the Balkans and now called Turkey-in-Europe. Salonica, where so many of the Young Turks had cut their teeth, was Greek.

The Balkan Wars ended in the summer of 1913, but that did not stop the threatened unravelling, even of the heartlands. One sign was that Albania, long a great buttress of the empire, became independent in December 1913: the only sign, today, of that long, buccaneering presence being the existence in Istanbul of two places called Arnavutköy, 'Albanian village'. However, by now there were more dangerous threats. The Kurds had been almost an eastern equivalent of the Albanians – also fiercely tribal and divided, but also ferociously loyal. At this point, some of the chieftains, who had acquired sophistication in Constantinople, began to see some sense in a nationalism of their own; the Russians, especially, took an interest and were first off the mark when it came to study of the Kurdish language (or, more accurately, languages). The Arabs also produced a nationalism of sorts – led, generally, by the Christians among them, who could look to the French and, now, the British in Egypt for interest and support. A long war had to be fought in the Yemen as well.

However, the greatest threat was posed by the Armenians. There was still a substantial Armenian population in the six eastern Anatolian provinces of historic Armenia, although it was nowhere a majority. The Ottoman collapse in the Balkans and North Africa presaged an overall collapse, and Armenian nationalists tapped their feet; in this, at last, they received encouragement from Russia. Weapons were smuggled across the border, and Russian consuls offered support in other ways; in the Caucasus, Tsarist governors had been very suspicious of the Armenians, partly on the grounds that, in Baku and elsewhere, being good at business, they complicated relations with the Muslim Tatars (as the Azeris were then known).

Kars, reconstructed since 1878 as a Russian provincial town, topped by its enormous and grand citadel, had become nine-tenths Armenian, the Muslims known only as porters and itinerant tradesmen, and Armenian nationalists now dreamed of it as the capital of a restored country.

Russian policy in these matters was very far from straightforward. Yes, Christian Greater Armenia might be a useful tool; but equally she might look west, and especially to the British, who were carefully examining the oil of nearby Iran and Iraq; and besides, there were the Kurds, some of whom acted in concert with Russians, but who had their own quarrels with Armenians. Yes, again, the seizure of Constantinople, the flying once more of the Double Eagle in the Second Rome, was supposed to be a Russian dream. But what might happen if the Greeks, encouraged by the British, took the city instead? Prudent Russians therefore calculated that their interests were best served by a weak Turkey. In that sense, they produced a scheme, not for Armenian independence, but for a 'reform' that would leave the six provinces with a Christian governor and foreign police chiefs, but still within Turkey. The scheme was carefully argued, and the Russian hand was not shown – on the contrary, the foreigners were chosen among neutrals – such that the other Great Powers did not object. The Turks were forced to accept the scheme early in 1914 (although it was never ratified). As a sign of goodwill they even offered a job in the Cabinet to the Armenian leader, Boghos Nubar, who refused on the grounds that his Turkish was not up to it.

Into all of this stepped a German general. In the spring of 1913, the Young Turks asked for a German military mission to be sent, to reform the army. After weary negotiations, mainly as to the salaries, some seventy officers arrived in December 1913 at Sirkeci station, at the European end of the Orient Express. At their head was one Liman von Sanders, son of a converted Jew and therefore supposed, in wooden Prussian thinking, to be suitable for that Orient (he also had an English wife). A German general, in command of a Turkish army corps at the Straits? For Russia, here was a vital interest: 90 per cent of her grain exports – and she was at that time the greatest grain-exporter in the world – went through those selfsame Straits, quite apart from the strategic interests involved. This was the first direct German-Russian quarrel, and it ended with a ragged compromise only in the following March. Liman stayed on, and some of his officers behaved with such stiff-necked arrogance that both the German ambassador and even the driving civilian force among the young Turks, Talât Bey (then minister of the interior, but soon to become grand vizier, with the rank of pasha) solemnly wrote to Berlin to have the mission withdrawn. But there were powerful German interests at work – the Deutsche Bank, funding the Berlin–Baghdad railway – and an idea was going the rounds in Berlin, that Turkey could become 'Our Egypt'. The French might have the bulk of investment, but the Germans and Austrians had most of the trade, and were squeezing out the British.

By now, everyone had written off the Turks: the question was, how would the empire be partitioned, oil and all? In this, the Balkans mattered, because they were quite literally in and on the way. Earlier, the partition of China had caused great rivalry among the Great Powers, but that had involved navies, not armies, and in any case the historic interests were not involved. Ottoman Turkey, the Middle East and the Balkans were quite different. So long as Russia had been weak and backward, as, say, the Crimean War and even the war of 1877–78 had shown, there was at least a balance. But since 1908 Russia had been booming, and by 1917, when her armaments and strategic railways would, according to plans, come up to scratch, she, in alliance with France, would be a match for Germany.

From the time of the Liman von Sanders crisis, you can see panic growing in Berlin, the generals pounding on the table: war now, before it is too late. The chancellor, Theobald von Bethmann Hollweg, told this to his private secretary, who recorded it in his diary. But how do you find an excuse for war? One turned up, when the heir to the crowns of Austria-Hungary was shot by a Serb terrorist at Sarajevo in Bosnia. The Germans told their Austro-Hungarian ally to provoke a war with Serbia; then, when the Russians responded with a mobilization of their forces, to protect their own Balkan position, Berlin declared war; when France mobilized, war came there as well, and when military logic dictated a German invasion of Belgium, the British were also dragged in. By 4 August European war had broken out. What, now, were the Turks to do?

Some argued, to the point of resignation, for doing nothing, or taking up a British alliance. The problem here was that Turkey might then just have been partitioned, as part of some grand compromise-peace (and there had been something similar in the air after Napoleon and Alexander I had made their bargain at Tilsit in 1807). By an extraordinary coincidence, two German battleships managed to escape from a British hunt in the Mediterranean, and they arrived in the then neutral waters of the Straits. Already on 2 August the true masters of the government – other ministers were not informed – had made their own arrangements for a German alliance: Talât, the grand vizier Said Halim Pasha, and the military chief, Enver Pasha, had signed the document in the garden of the German ambassador's summer house at Tarabya, some way up the Bosphorus towards the Black Sea. The document was kept secret.

Now, an ingenious way was found to defeat the British: the two German ships, SMS *Goeben* and *Breslau*, were turned over to the Ottoman navy, the crews wearing fezzes, and the commanding admiral, Wilhelm Souchon, entering Turkish service. Here was a wonderful shortcut to create a properly independent Turkey, to defy the restrictions placed on her by the western Powers. Enver thought up a way of provoking war. He sent the German ships into the Black Sea, where they were more powerful than anything afloat, and these bombarded the Russian port of Odessa, causing much damage. The Russians, perplexed, diplomatically enquired what had happened; an unsatisfactory response followed, and by early November Turkey was at war with Britain, France and Russia – a coalition soon joined by Italy. By 1916, these four had worked out arrangements for the very partition of the empire that this war had been supposed to forestall.

Enver was an adventurer by nature, and his pattern so far had been last-minute rabbit-out-of-hat success. He was still very young – his career of extraordinary destruction ended in 1922 when he was only just forty – and he gambled, first of all on a short war (that was an almost universal illusion, in retrospect the worst of them all) and then on an agreed peace, in which Turkey might recover Salonica. The Young Turks had one immediate advantage, which all Turks by now wanted: an end to the Capitulations, the extraordinary privileges taken by the western Powers in matters economic. These, with reluctant German assent, were indeed abolished, and the Turks could therefore run their own economy at last. This favoured the emergence of a national commercial class, and as a mark of this, a law was passed to compel businesses to transact their affairs in Turkish.

Enver had also gambled on international Islam. The Young Turks' religious chief solemnly intoned Holy War. It did not help that he was a freemason, nor that the Holy War meant enlisting one set of Christians against another set; but in any case the appeal was hollow, and made no troubles among Indian Muslims (the Emir of Afghanistan, solemnly presented with the appeal by some enterprising Germans, more or less made a paper dart out of it) or Russian Tatars. More immediately, it had no effect in Egypt, and a fanciful attack on the Suez Canal got nowhere. Enver had also gambled on a Russian collapse in the Caucasus, and drove his Third Army into snowy plateau territory west of Kars. The communications to the east were terrible, as the Baghdad railway went only as far as Ankara, and troops had to be marched all the five hundred miles beyond that. Essential weaponry could only come from Germany, herself under pressure, and links across the Balkans were also strained; 90,000 men were lost at the time of the battle of Sarıkamış in December 1914.

Then comes an extraordinary moment of Turkish recovery – a repetition, on a larger scale, of what had happened in the first months of 1913. The British, Churchill in the lead, had calculated that Turkey would collapse if a naval effort were made against the Dardanelles, and in March 1915 they, with a French contribution, sent twelve great battleships into the Straits, armed with big guns. However, mobile shore batteries could be concealed, and these did damage; so did mines. Three battleships were sunk, and another three were badly damaged; the British withdrew. Then they tried a landing, on the coast of the Gallipoli peninsula, and a battle went on there until February 1916, when an evacuation took place. These schemes only made sense on the assumption that the Turks would collapse, and there was indeed panic in Constantinople. But this was another of those war illusions. Amphibious operations in an age of modern weaponry were horribly difficult, as men emerging from landing craft could easily be put out of action by safely hidden shore artillery or even just by well-aimed rifles; the landing force could not be easily supplied, even with elementary essentials such as water; and the ordinary Turkish soldier, whatever his weak points as regards overenthusiastic attack, did not know the meaning of the word panic.

Only two men on the British side understood this: one of them, Aubrey Herbert, who had been all round the Ottoman Empire and knew the languages (he was offered, and turned down, the crown of Albania), and the other, a Colonel Doughty-Wylie, who had served as military consul in Adana with a view to pacifying the situation as regards the Armenians in 1909, had greatly sympathized with the Turks to the point of serving with the Red Crescent, equivalent to the Red Cross, had been decorated by the Sultan, and now, landing with the troops in April 1915, carried only a swagger stick, as he did not intend to kill Turks (he was himself shot, but was awarded a posthumous VC). Otherwise, on the British side, overconfidence, romanticism and glorious inefficiency reigned. The attacks failed; an attempt in August at a landing further up the coast also failed. With 250,000 casualties on the Allied side, and perhaps 400,000 on the Turkish, the Allies withdrew to Salonica, where another front – in violation of Greek neutrality – was set up, though not, until 1918, to any effect. In the spring of 1916 there was another Turkish victory, at Kut-el-Amara south of Baghdad, where a British division was besieged and had to surrender.

The British attacks in March–April 1915 made for a deadly threat, and coincided with Russian attacks in eastern Anatolia. The Constantinople government responded with a deadly measure. The Armenian situation now became acute. There were four Armenian brigades in the Russian army, and the Patriarch in Russian Armenia, with endorsement from the Tsar, appealed for a general rising against the Turks. This duly occurred in the area of Van, where Muslims were slaughtered, and the Muslim town, at the foot of the great rock-fortress overlooking Lake Van, was smashed (you can still see the vestiges).

There were also attacks, late in April, on the rear communications and the exiguous signalling equipment of the Turkish army. This coincided with the Allied landings at Gallipoli, and Talât responded, rounding up the leading Armenian figures in Constantinople, who were deported to the interior and in some cases killed. Then came orders for deportation of the Armenian population of the military area (many exceptions were made) and columns of civilians trudged towards areas of settlement elsewhere, mainly in northern Syria. There were attacks on these columns, by Kurdish or Arab tribes, in some cases in collusion with the Ottoman authorities, and there were well-documented massacres, observed by foreign consuls and by missionaries, who assumed that this was all happening by government order. This has never been directly proven – the evidence is now generally accepted as forged – and the government even put some 1,500 of its own men on trial, executing fifty, including a governor.

Was this 'genocide', a claim that is so often made? As the historian Bernard Lewis says, it depends on what you mean by the word; and if it is accepted for the events of 1915, it could legitimately be extended to cover the fates of the millions of Muslims driven from the Balkans or the Caucasus as the Ottoman Empire receded. The Armenians of Constantinople, Smyrna and Aleppo were left alone, but there were grubby tales elsewhere. In Ankara or Kayseri, there were substantial Armenian populations, doing no one any harm. They had property, sometimes substantial. They too were deported, and associates of the CUP stole the properties, to their families' subsequent and often significant enrichment.

By 1917, the military effort was causing vast hardship. Desertion occurred, and banditry followed. There was an uncountable price-inflation, and even proud dignitaries were reduced to wearing heavily patched clothing; there was widespread starvation and disease. Whole areas of eastern Anatolia were almost emptied of people, and as the Russian army took swathes of territory, including Erzurum and Trebizond, there were further massacres by the Armenians. The empire was saved from collapse only by the inactivity of the Allies' Salonica army on the one side, and then, on the other, by the Russian Revolution. In March 1917 the Tsar was overthrown, and in November the Bolsheviks took over, with a programme of Bread, Peace and Land (to the peasant) of which Peace, at any rate, could be realized. An armistice came in December 1917, and a treaty, at the German headquarters' town of Brest-Litovsk, in March 1918.

All of a sudden, Enver Pasha's schemes now seemed to make sense. The Russians withdrew from the southern Caucasus, and Enver sent in his troops, as far as Baku on the Caspian (and even further north), where there was an Azeri population, inclined to sympathize with the Turks. An independent Armenia came into shadowy existence as well, compelled, for the moment, to come to terms with the Turks. However, this was all illusion. In France, the German army launched a set of spectacular offensives, which failed by July 1918; there followed successful Allied offensives, which brought the Germans to ask for an armistice in November. Before then, their allies had also collapsed – first Bulgaria, late in September. The Turks were now cut off from Germany, and the government disintegrated (the chief CUP men fleeing on a German torpedo boat to a warship and then Odessa, which was still under the control of the Central Powers). The Turks approached the British naval commander in the Aegean for an armistice, signed on 30 October at Mudros, on the island of Lemnos (and partly through the good offices of the British general captured at Kut-el-Amara,

Sir Charles Vere Townshend, who had had a comfortable internment on Büyükada – in Greek *Prinkipo* from the word for prince – the largest island off Istanbul, where, subsequently, Trotsky was also to be semi-interned). An Allied occupation of Constantinople followed.

The victors meant now to divide up the empire: Italians in the south-west, British in Iraq, Palestine and the Constantinople region, the French all over Syria and the south-east. There were proxies. Armenians now dreamed of a Greater Armenia, from the Black Sea to the Mediterranean, and they claimed some American support. There was a further possibility: Kurdestan. Of course the Powers quarrelled among themselves, and the British decided to use the Greeks, whose prime minister, the nationalist Venizelos, was greatly admired and trusted by Lloyd George especially. In mid-May 1919 they were encouraged to occupy partly Greek Smyrna and their troops spread out over that area, expelling the Turks and behaving sometimes with much cruelty (one of their army commanders, Prince Andrew, father of the Duke of Edinburgh, said that he had not believed any human beings could behave in this way, let alone Greeks).

Meanwhile, the Sultan, now Mehmet VI Vahdettin (r. 1918–22), and his cronies were defeatist. The Ottomans had after all tried everything – *Tanzimat* secularization, a constitution, co-operation over the Debt, Islamic reaction, revolution of a sort, alliance with Britain, alliance with Germany: nothing had worked. The Sultan saw a future only as Caliph, Muslim figurehead for the entire world, including, of course, British India, where he thought he still held some trumps. In other words, he would become a sort of Aga Khan (head of a civilized variant of Islam and also very rich). His men signed the Treaty of Sèvres, in 1920, which carved up the empire and left him with a small state in central Anatolia, the capital of which might even have been Ankara. It was a humiliating treaty, designed to bring civilization to the Turks, who undertook to grease the brakes on locomotives and not to sell dirty postcards. In the Smyrna region, a governor was moved in, Aristidis Stergiadis, who, as a Cretan, was supposed to understand Muslims and who had been the first Greek governor of occupied Salonica. His ways were in fact mild, mild enough to enrage the local Greek nationalists. The Greeks even set up a university of the eastern Mediterranean, meant to re-Hellenize the local Muslims. Meanwhile, the Armenians occupied Kars, and drove towards Trebizond and Erzurum; their megalomania was such that their first action after the armistice was to attack Georgia, on the grounds that Batum, a considerable port, really belonged to them.

All of this brought a Muslim reaction – we can fairly call it 'Turkish', but at the time ordinary locals, especially in the east, would have defined themselves by religion. A leader of genius now emerged, Mustafa Kemal, whom the world knows from his later, adopted, name, as Atatürk, or 'Father of the Turks'. He had been a very successful general, at Gallipoli and elsewhere, and he played a careful game, initially getting approval from the Sultan (who maybe suspected what he was really about) and then departing on a pretext and on a Clyde-built steamer to Samsun, on the Black Sea, on 19 May 1919. Travelling along the dusty roads in an abandoned German staff car (which frequently broke down) he rallied support. The Armenians, who had been massacring quite diligently on their own account, caused the Muslims, including Kurds, to unite as they might never otherwise have done, and Mustafa Kemal had the charisma and the cunning to become their leader. Then he challenged the Sultan's government. By chance he hit upon Ankara as his base, because it was on a railway line and because it had a telegraph office, which he used to great effect. Soon, Mustafa Kemal was collecting adherents from occupied Constantinople, and a 'Grand National Assembly' met in April 1920 in the clubhouse of the Young Turks. It was no rubber stamp; running it was difficult, and great concessions had to be made (such as a prohibition on alcohol and religious provisions for women's dress). However, there was in existence an army, which had retreated from the Caucasus, and though the French in the south-east, with an Armenian legion in tow, and the Greeks in the west advanced, there was gathering resistance to them.

In 1920 a new factor entered the calculations. In Russia the Bolsheviks had won the civil war, but they greatly feared an Allied intervention, and they needed support. They had come to understand that, under the banner of anti-imperialism, they could recruit Muslims; and after some experimentation with Enver, they somehow guessed that Mustafa Kemal would be their man. Messages went between Ankara and Moscow, followed by envoys, and a deal was done. In 1920 Soviet gold and arms came over the Black Sea, and the first effect was felt on the eastern front, where the Armenians collapsed. Then the nationalists sent support to the south-eastern front, where the French soon came to terms, and also did a deal over the Syrian border. By 1921, the Turks had enough strength to resist the Greeks who, sure of British support, advanced wildly towards Ankara. At a great battle on the Sakarya river, in August–September, they were stopped, and it was a victory that ran round the world, especially the Muslim world: telegrams of congratulation came from all sides.

Mustafa Kemal then showed his qualities in another way: he knew when to stop. He did not want to provoke British intervention, and refrained, for a year, from attacking; instead (and this needed management) he built up his domestic position in Ankara, which was acquiring the rudiments of a capital (the French embassy was the railway buffet). Then in August 1922 he attacked, and this time it was the Greeks' turn to collapse. Their army broke (even the high command was captured) and on 9 September the Turks entered Smyrna (which subsequently became İzmir). The Greeks, retreating, had set fire to various places, and there were, in the great bay, some thirty Allied warships. Smyrna contained about 300,000 Greeks and other Christians, and the Turkish general, Nurettin, in any event an embittered, not to say maddened, man who had lost his sons in this war, probably decided to prevent any reconquest. The non-Muslim (and non-Jewish: on the whole the Jews had taken the nationalist side) part of the city was burned, in a fire that lasted for five days, while hundreds of thousands of refugees clustered on the coastal road and the harbour, waiting for help that diplomatic niceties did not allow for all of that time. It is an episode that has entered the world's subconscious. At any rate, the nationalists had won. Mustafa Kemal entered the city, and found that, on the steps of the government house, a Greek flag had been draped for him to walk over. He would not: chivalry meant that he had to respect a flag for which men had died.

In the event, his forces moved on Constantinople, and there encountered a British cordon. Lloyd George was adamant that the Turks could not be allowed to win, and sent a telegram to the local commander, ordering him to fight. The commander, 'Tim' Harington, was a man of great common sense and humanity; in any case the British army had come to respect the Turks and, as it turned out, some of the survivors of Kut-el-Amara even spent their summer holidays, years later, with their old guards. Harington kept the telegram in his pocket and pretended that it had not arrived. Then he negotiated sensibly with the Turks, agreeing to let them into what is now Turkey-in-Europe, and, in November, into Constantinople. The Sultan, fearing the worst, was smuggled onto a British warship and taken, with his five wives, to Malta (where he was presented with a bill). In 1923, a peace treaty followed, at Lausanne, and it established Turkey's present-day borders, although these were extended, in 1939, when the French handed back the area of Antakya, the old Antioch, which had originally been assigned to their Syrian colony. Then, in 1923 and 1924, came the crowning and dismal consequence of all of this. Hatred between Turks and Greeks had of course grown and grown, and co-existence was hardly possible. An exchange of populations followed: about half a million Muslims, some of them Greek-speaking, from Greece, and about a million Greeks, many Turkish-speaking, from Anatolia. Misery followed, and both countries were set back a generation, although in Constantinople itself about a quarter of a million Greeks were permitted to go on residing with their Patriarch in the old Fener district. But by now a separate and national Turkish state had been established, and Mustafa Kemal proclaimed it a republic on 29 October 1923.

EPILOGUE

The Turkish Republic

There was one final Ottoman moment, and it was a sign of things to come, much later on. There was always a strong religious element to Turkish nationalism, and Kemal Atatürk was very careful not to alienate it. He had a fight even to have the Sultan deposed, and he made a concession: the Sultan's cousin, Abdülmecit, was initially allowed to stay on in the Dolmabahçe Palace as Caliph of all Islam – in any case, the Republic was still very weak, and here at least was a card to brandish. However, Atatürk, as we can now call him, was set on eliminating Islam from public life, and the first step was to depose the Caliph as well, who, with over a hundred members of the Ottoman dynasty, was expelled in 1924. There was much muttering about this, and in 1926 a political trial was staged against some surviving Young Turks who objected particularly to the end of the caliphate and the downgrading of religion; others, including one-time close associates, were sent into exile. There was also a Kurdish rebellion, put down with great force. Still, Atatürk's prestige was such that no one would now attack him, and he went on to form, in effect, a one-party state.

Kemal Atatürk himself became the object of a cult, his statue in every village – like Lenin – and he does not seem to have objected. It continues to this day, often to the bewilderment of foreigners. But Atatürk stands for a code: a modern Turkey, set apart from primitive neighbours, in which women are equal, and westernization is the goal. In the 1920s and 1930s, reforms went ahead. The greatest of them concerned language, the scrapping, in a month at the end of 1928, of the old Ottoman Arabo-Persian alphabet which was no doubt poetic but could never be used as a vehicle for the mass literacy that Turkey went on to achieve with Latin letters. The language reform also involved eliminating some of the Arabic or Persian vocabulary, and although this was defensible in the early 1930s – no 'Turk' would have understood such words – it went far too far later on, resulting in a mutilation of the language such that students of today have to have yesterday's classics rendered into ultra-modern Turkish. Even the constitution had to be translated, and then the 1924 one restored after a different government was elected in 1950.

It was in this context that the old university was disbanded and a thousand foreign scholars hired to staff the new one – a matter that still divides the jury. Foreign models in medicine, education and architecture were followed, and Ankara itself was built up quite quickly as a capital city, with some decent Bauhaus-style buildings, broad streets, an opera, a theatre, a state library, an English-language school. Although later on it was almost swamped by rural migrants, and although the Istanbul people regard it as bureaucratically boring, it still works quite well, and is a good place for a young family. The symbol of all of this was Atatürk's insistence that men should wear hats, not fezzes or turbans; and he did not like beards, either. Between the two world wars there was considerable progress of the then approved sort, and there was a small tidal wave of adulatory books. There was also much imitation, whether in Afghanistan or Persia and even, later, by Nasser in Egypt.

Islam at that time was simply written off as a burden – illiteracy, mindless conservatism, and endless wastes of money on gifts to saints' tombs and the like. Such extravagance was banned, along with the various brotherhoods (*tarikat*) that encouraged them, except partly for the Mevlevi, historically much more tolerant and open (even the great minister of education of the 1940s, Hasan Ali Yücel, who used to hold court on western literature at a cafe in Tandoğan, near Ankara University, was a Mevlevi). The Koran was now translated into Turkish and the call to prayer was also performed in

Turkish, not Arabic. In public Atatürk was very careful, but in private (and he did drink too much) he would say how absurd it was for a seventh-century Beduin to be dictating the smallest details of people's personal lives. Religious conservatives hated all of this, but could not speak out openly. Their time was to come later, and they spoke the language of the persecutor with the tones of the persecuted, as someone had said of Pope Pius IX, once he had been deprived of his monopoly of education in Italy in the mid-nineteenth century.

In one matter, Atatürk was again careful. Jews, Armenians and Greeks were still far more prominent in important parts of the economy than their numbers could justify: Greeks accounted for half of the stock exchange. In the 1920s, when the world made an effort to return to the free trade and stable currencies of 1914, the minorities were still all-important. However, in the world slump of 1929, foreign trade and investment crashed, and there was not much alternative to state action. The Republicans then had to set up marketing boards and new national industries; in this, they got Soviet help. In 1929 Trotsky was expelled by a Stalin who was not yet powerful enough just to have him killed, as would happen later on. The Turks agreed to take him, and he lived for four years on the island of Büyükada (in the hideous house built for İzzet Pasha, Abdülhamit's hatchet man). The counterpart seems to have been a soft loan of 8 million gold roubles and several textile factories, especially one at Kayseri, where the local elite was strongly republican-nationalist and where – it is almost the dead centre of the country – there are now aircraft and furniture industries, and a certain difficulty in obtaining a drink. The old Armenian church lives on, and there is the obvious hulk of a Greek school, but the old quarters were pulled down for a mass of concrete that embraces the grand Seljuk buildings of yesteryear.[1]

1 The eleventh president of the Republic, Abdullah Gül, elected in 2007, comes from there and incorporates in his person the Kayseri of today. It is successfully industrial, but it is also quite strictly religious, and symbolizes the emergence, since Özal's time, of an Anatolian capitalism with which the republican and secular elements have a difficult relationship.

A Soviet official visit in 1933 was marked by naming a 'Voroshilov Square' in rebuilt İzmir after the Soviet general.

In those years, if you turned on the radio, you heard only western classical music; football, Boy Scouts, were in evidence, though the Scouts were run by the ministry of education; a Turkish opera singer, Semiha Berksoy, became famous in Europe, and the Turks were well established on the international scene. Atatürk died, vastly respected, in 1938. As time has gone by, his legend has of course been contested, as has happened with a comparable figure, de Gaulle. Both men took the credit for subordinates' achievements; both persecuted deserving underlings quite unnecessarily; both might be accused of imposing solutions by authority, whereas more evolution might have been desirable. But they leave a sense of greatness just the same.

Atatürk's successors were not of the same class. To start with, they clung rigidly to the republican formula, and the police became vastly resented because of bullying and pettiness. During the war, through most of which Turkey remained neutral, the economy suffered very badly from shortages and inflation, as so many of the young men were kept under arms. There was much hostility towards the minorities, and an effort was made in 1942 to make them pay, to compensate for the dreadful penury. This – the property tax or *varlık vergisi* – turned out to be a lesser version of the discrimination against minorities that became horribly prevalent in many countries of the Europe of that period. It was a bad mistake. Several businesses went bankrupt in consequence (there was even a tax-paying category, 'D', standing for *Dönme*, i.e. descended from the Jewish converts to Islam) and there were grubby profiteers. That tax was scrapped early in 1944, but it did damage to Turkey's reputation. More damage came from the then president İsmet İnönü's refusal to join the Allies in 1943, when Churchill especially asked for this. İnönü was desperately prudent, and feared, perhaps rightly, that if he did join, he might have to be rescued by the Soviet Union and the country would be taken over by Communists.

In the event, Turkey did join the West, but only because Joseph Stalin threatened her at the end of the war, demanding back the eastern provinces that had been ceded in 1918, and rights to garrison the Straits near Istanbul. At that, the Americans sent warships, and Turkey eventually benefited from the Marshall Plan. She joined NATO in 1952, having sent a contingent to the Korean War in 1950, and in the 1950s American aid flowed: tractors appeared in the countryside, and so did electricity. There was a political counterpart. The Americans preferred their allies to be democratic, and İnönü gave way. In 1950 he allowed a free election, and the single republican party was resoundingly defeated. A new party, the Democrats, emerged, and it made an approach to religion – not, at first, dramatic, but a sign of things to come. It was supported by Turkish and Muslim businessmen, and in 1955 came the worst mistake of modern Turkish history, when shady interests of this sort caused riots against the Greeks of Istanbul. They mainly left, as did many Armenians and Jews, much to the impoverishment of the country, and almost to the ruin of the old European centre, Beyoğlu and Galata, which have only recovered in the past ten or so years (the restoration is now spectacular). The Democrats then became both corrupt and authoritarian; they presided over an inflation, which made army officers poor; they became hated in enlightened, secular circles; they were overthrown by a military coup in 1960, and their prime minister, Adnan Menderes, was hanged, despite pleas from the Pope, President Eisenhower and the Queen of England. Even the Greek Patriarch had acted as a witness on his behalf. Turkey's international reputation did not recover for a long time.

Besides, the military coup solved nothing. Here was a poor country, and one with a terrible demographic problem. The republican progress of the 1930s had had a strong medical aspect, such that babies no longer died early on from lack of hygiene. Now, a country of 17 million added to itself the population of Denmark every year, and the village came to the town. Istanbul shot up from 1 million to (now) 15 million; Ankara from 400,000 to 4 million, and the outskirts of both were distinguished by mile upon mile of hastily built shacks. In the mainly Kurdish east, the problem was even worse, because, there, polygamy still flourished, and a man might have forty children, while even standard families produced a football team. These problems swamped education, electricity, sewage – everything. The makers of the military coup had imagined that they could deal with such problems if they had a properly functioning democracy, and they produced a constitution to that effect. New elections were held, under a system of proportional representation, and a Five Year Plan was started (still, now largely unnoticed, in existence).

This dream of westernization-by-wishful-thinking was soon checked. The electoral system merely showed the country's divisions, and these persist. There was a Left, dominated by republican secularists who had the sympathy of the army, and supported in the main by the Alevis, Muslims who were so heretical as hardly to count as Muslims at all. Then there was a Right, with provincial businessmen who were inclined towards religion; and there were two further smaller groups, an Islamic one with its roots in pious Konya, and a nationalist one, which sometimes talked outright Fascist language. Turkish political history in the 1960s is unhappy, the more so as a younger generation of secularist know-alls espoused terrorism. At Robert College, by now a venerable place of education, the problem was such that the portraits of the American founders were taken down and the police had to be called in: it was at this point that the college moved and the buildings were given over to Boğaziçi University.

In 1971 there was a further military coup, but the pattern was re-imposed, and the politics of the 1970s, bedevilled by inflation, debt and shortages of energy, were still more dismal. By 1979, about twenty people were being killed every day in battles between Left, Right and Islamists, and major universities became battlegrounds. In 1960, Turkey had been well ahead of South Korea, the chief export of which had been wigs. Twenty years later, there was a Korean miracle, with worldwide products, whereas Turkey was still exporting tomatoes. In 1980 came another military coup, this time much better thought through than earlier such exercises. The generals had perhaps learned, via the CIA, from the example of General Pinochet in Chile in 1973. He had taken power in a swoop, had decreed free-market reforms, had presided over a considerable economic recovery, and had then held an election which he lost.

The Turkish generals did not go so far. In the first place, the casualties of this coup were very few in number, although there was an enormous outcry, and maybe 1,500 people went into exile. Most of the country received news of the coup with a sigh of relief. The generals themselves did not want political prominence, as distinct from behind-the-scenes influence, and they were not particularly interested in free markets: they only wanted the economy to work better. Besides, their American and European allies were adamant that democracy should be restored. They arrested the old politicians (quite humanely: they got the men's best friends to press the 3 a.m. doorbell, fearing that, if politicians of the standard Turkish political size saw soldiers at the door, there might be heart attacks) and banned the old parties.

In 1982 new parties emerged, and one of them, Motherland, was able, as the outcome of clever manoeuvring, to present itself as the true opposition. Its leader was Turgut Özal, and he was the second maker of the republic. He was the Americans' man, having served in the World Bank, and when his party won the elections of 1983 and 1987, his cabinets contained members with American doctorates. Özal was a man for economic liberalization, and Turkey's strategic place in the Middle East, then boiling over, meant that she could rely on the International Monetary Fund and the World Trade Organization for help. The outcome, together with liberalization of trade and financial dealings, was a rush of energy which made for something of an economic miracle. It was export-led, and was based on the elements that had made for such miracles elsewhere – devaluation, a scrapping of currency controls, greater freedom for banks, labour mobility, (on the whole) low taxes. By 2010 Turkey's had become the twentieth economy of the world – a long, long way from the days when, if you wanted a table made, you had to have an Armenian carpenter who would understand how to stop the legs from wobbling. The roads – very good ones – from Istanbul to Kayseri and Antep were studded with heavy lorries moving goods to Central Europe; one in four televisions sold in the UK were made in Turkey; salesmen for Turkish pharmaceutical companies were all over the world.

Özal died relatively young, unable to control his eating and smoking, in 1993, but he had remade the republic. One element of that was a dismantling of the old state machine. It went on, but was overtaken by private money. Discipline now came from an odd source. The army, seizing power in 1980, had deliberately made a compact with the clergy, or at any rate some elements among them. As an antidote to Marxism, and also to the Maoist Kurdish separatists of the PKK, Islam was powerful, and it made an appearance in the schools, where religious instruction became compulsory. The special schools designed to train the clergy were also expanded in number, far beyond the original purpose, and in secular eyes, these institutions brainwashed boys and especially girls into accepting age-old roles that meant backwardness, nastiness and stupidity. But there was a problem over this, in that the secular-minded governments outdid themselves in corruption and inefficiency.

The Islamic party, by contrast, acted in the main honestly and efficiently, as Recep Tayyip Erdoğan's period in office (1994–98) as mayor of Istanbul showed (he subsequently became prime minister). Previous governments had been unable to deal with a note inflation of ridiculous proportions (at the end, before currency reform in 2005, there was a fifty million note, equivalent to £20). It was not a real inflation, in the sense that you could switch your money in and out of dollars at the press of a button or two, and prices in dollars were going up only slightly. The system profited the government, which produced the paper and then switched into dollars; this made up for tax revenue that was inefficiently collected, and the gap in time between a person's receiving Turkish millions and turning them into American tens was such that a per cent or two went to the government as a sort of arbitrage profit. Meanwhile, anyone with money could, by timing money-changing, make a 25 per cent tax-free profit very easily, just through a bank's managed fund. The people who suffered were those working for the state, who paid income tax, and of course the poor, who showed extraordinary resignation, though crime rates did begin to go up. In the 1990s and 2000s, the rich, especially in Istanbul, were very rich indeed; one lady was reported returning from a shopping expedition to London in 2008 with twenty-seven suitcases.

This was the background to the election, in 2002, of an Islamic-led government, though it was one with a difference, in that it proclaimed toleration, and did indeed, at least in places under foreign scrutiny, tolerate alcohol and irreligiously dressed women in ways that would have been abhorrent to the party's much more rigid forerunners. That the Americans and the Europeans greatly approved of this experiment in Muslim democracy of course helped, and Turkey's reward was supposed to be membership of the European Union. That opened up the old question, going back to the post-Tamerlane period, when the Ottoman court spoke Greek, and some of the Turkish elite had looked to the Aegean and towards Renaissance Italy for alliance. In those days the Anatolian east had won, and now there is the question of the Kurds. Get rid of them, and Turkey is a Greece and perhaps even a sort of late Byzantium, in thrall to latter-day Latins in the form of the European Union, which would probably accept as a member a Turkey that was essentially a sort of greater Istanbul. Keep the Kurds, and the best answer becomes neo-Hamidian: the politicization of religion. Heads are shaken over this, not least among Kurds, who do not like Ottomanism and prefer, in millions, a western Turkey that works. In any case, there is, under way, one of the largest energy schemes in the world – the GAP, or 'South-eastern Anatolian Project', which has built large dams, and will create more, to bring hydroelectricity and irrigation to a part of the world that has never really recovered from the doings of Tamerlane. It has already caused a greening of vast areas, and we shall see whether it succeeds.

On economic grounds, the case for Europe was easily made. This was also true with politics. Was not the new religious party (the AKP) just a variant of the Christian Democracy that had run Italy more or less without a break since 1947? It had presided over an economic miracle as well, and also by methods that were irregular, to say the least. In Italy, people stole from the state and the country was rich; in England, the state stole from the people, who were overtaken by Italians, who also had a much less put-upon life, at any rate until 'Europe' took a say in the sort of miniature bureaucratic persecution at which it excelled. On almost any grounds, Turkey was of far greater interest for Europe than all the other new members put together. However, the prospect of a vast Turkish and Kurdish migration, at a time when Islam was not popular and when economies were not growing, was a deterrent, and in any case, by characteristic ineptitude, the Europeans had allowed in Greek Cyprus before the problem of Turkish Cyprus had been resolved, and the Greeks could therefore obstruct Turkey's progress. Did this in any case matter very much? Trade and investment went ahead, and there were more interesting markets than saturated Europe.

In Turkey, there were, by 2010, serious difficulties between the old secular authorities and the new semi-religious ones, as judges and generals were arrested on this or that pretext. There were troubles in the south-east with Kurdish separatism (which did not affect the votes of the millions of Kurds living outside these provinces). But these things, or an identifiable equivalent, had been present in Turkish history since the *Tanzimat*, and even, in a way, before: that contest had to be lived with, and it was not going to lead to orgies of killings, as these phenomena had done in Spain, whether under the Napoleonic occupation or in the Civil War of the 1930s. And the new factor was simply prosperity. Turkey had become an important place again, and, be it said, the only country between Athens and Singapore where, judging by the refugees, people actually wanted to live.

THE OTTOMAN EMPIRE AT ITS GREATEST EXTENT, 1683

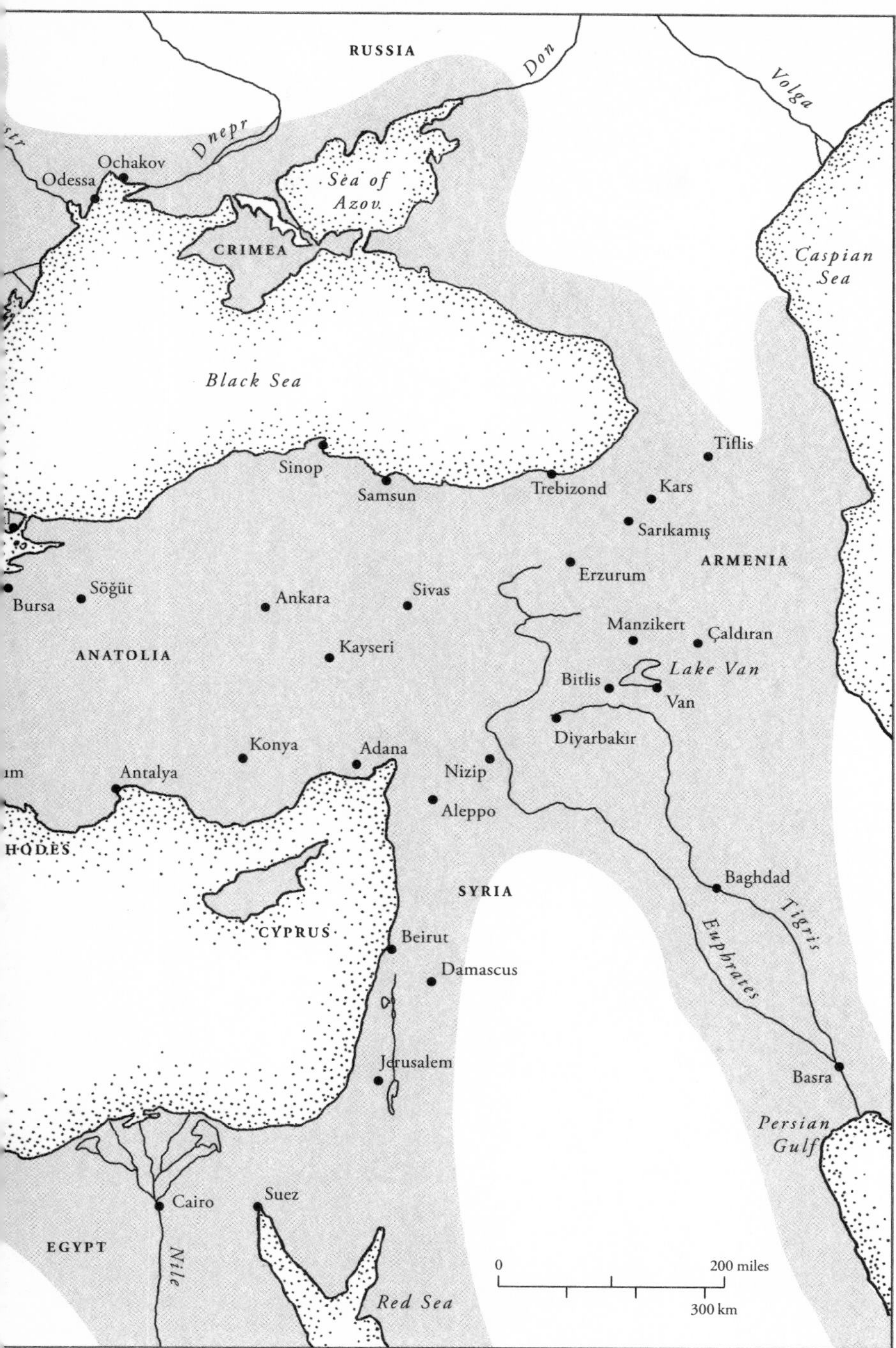
RUSSIA
Don
Volga
Dnepr
Ochakov
Odessa
Sea of Azov
CRIMEA
Caspian Sea
Black Sea
Tiflis
Sinop
Samsun
Trebizond
Kars
Sarıkamış
ARMENIA
Erzurum
Söğüt
Bursa
Ankara
Sivas
Manzikert
Çaldıran
ANATOLIA
Kayseri
Lake Van
Bitlis
Van
Diyarbakır
Konya
Adana
Antalya
Nizip
Aleppo
SYRIA
Baghdad
Tigris
Euphrates
CYPRUS
Beirut
Damascus
Jerusalem
Basra
Persian Gulf
Cairo
Suez
EGYPT
Nile
Red Sea
0
200 miles
300 km

CHRONOLOGY

SULTANS	DATES	KEY EVENTS
	1071	Battle of Manzikert: Seljuk Turks defeat Byzantine army
	1204	Crusaders sack Constantinople
Osman I	1324	Death of first Sultan
Orhan I *c. 1324–62*	1326	Ottomans capture Bursa
Murat I *c. 1362–89*	1389	Battle of Kosovo: Lazar of Serbia defeated; Murat assassinated
Bayezit I *1389–1402*	1396	Battle of Nikopol: Ottomans defeat Crusader army
	1402	Battle of Ankara: Tamerlane defeats Ottomans
Interregnum	1402–13	Sons of Bayezit vie for control
Mehmet I *1413–21*	1413–21	Mehmet reconstitutes Bayezit's empire
Murat II *1421–51*	1444	Ottomans defeat Crusaders at Varna
Mehmet II	1453	Constantinople captured
1451–81	1454–82	Conquest of Serbia, Athens and the Morea, Trebizond, Bosnia, Wallachia, Albania and Herzegovina
Bayezit II *1481–1512*	1481	Revolt by Prince Cem

	1492	Spanish Jews find refuge with Ottomans
	1499–1502	Ottoman–Venetian war
	1501	Safavid state founded by Shah Ismail
	1511	*Kızılbaş* rising led by Şahkulu
Selim I 1512–20	1514	Battle of Çaldıran: Ottoman army routs Safavids
	1516–17	Selim takes Syria and Egypt
Süleyman I 1520–66	1521	Ottomans take Belgrade
	1522	Conquest of Rhodes
	1526	Hungarian resistance destroyed at Battle of Mohacs
	1529	Failure of siege of Vienna
	1565	Malta repels Ottoman forces
Selim II 1566–74	1571	Ottomans take Cyprus from Venice
	1571	Battle of Lepanto: Holy League defeats Ottomans
Murat III 1574–95	1589	Janissaries rebel
	1590s	Celali revolts begin in Anatolia
	1593–1606	War against the Habsburgs
Mehmet III 1595–1603	1595	By law of fratricide, Mehmet's nineteen brothers are strangled
Ahmet I 1603–1617	1609	Work begins on the Blue Mosque
Mustafa I 1617–18	1618	Thirty Years War starts in Europe

Osman II	1622	Osman II deposed and killed
1618–22		
Mustafa I	1623	Mustafa I deposed
1622–23		
Murat IV	1624	Baghdad lost to Safavids
1623–40	1638	Baghdad regained
İbrahim I	1644–69	War with Venice over Crete
1640–48	1648	İbrahim I deposed and killed
Mehmet IV	1651	Revolt of the guilds
1648–87	1656–61	Grand vizier Mehmet Köprülü stabilizes Ottoman rule
	1664	Ottoman defeat at Szentgotthárd
	1683	Siege of Vienna fails. Murder of grand vizier Kara Mustafa
Süleyman II	1688	Belgrade falls to Austrians
1687–91		
Ahmet II		
1691–95		
Mustafa II	1697	Ottomans lose Battle of Zenta
1695–1703	1699	Treaty of Karlowitz: Austria takes Hungary and Transylvania
Ahmet III	1718	Treaty of Passarowitz cedes Belgrade to Austria; 'time of tulips' begins
1703–30		
Mahmut I	1730	Succession of Mahmut I following Janissary revolt led by Patrona Halil brings 'time of tulips' to a close
1730–54		
Osman III		
1754–57		

Mustafa III 1757–74	1768–74	War with Catherine the Great of Russia
	1770	Russian naval victory at Çeşme
Abdülhamit I 1774–89	1774	Treaty of Küçük Kaynarca ends war
	1783	Russia annexes Crimea
	1787–92	War with Russia. Ochakov falls
Selim III 1789–1807	1798	Napoleon lands in Egypt
Mustafa IV 1807–8	1808	Murder of Selim III
Mahmut II 1808–39	1821–29	Greek War of Independence
	1826	Abolition of the Janissaries (the Auspicious Event)
	1827	Battle of Navarino: British and Russian fleets defeat Egyptian navy
	1831	Egyptians under İbrahim Pasha invade Syria
	1833	Treaty of Hünkâr İskelesi establishes Russian role in Ottoman affairs
	1838	Treaty of Balta Limanı opens free trade with Britain
	1839	Egyptian victory at battle of Nizip leads to recognition of Mehmet Ali as hereditary governor of Egypt
Abdülmecit I 1839–61	1839	Gülhane edict ushers in *Tanzimat*
	1848	Revolutions sweep Europe; Polish and Hungarian liberals arrive
	1853–56	Crimean War

Abdülaziz I 1861–76	1861	Imperial Ottoman Bank created
	1866	Uprising in Crete
	1875	Ottoman state bankrupt; rebellions in the Balkans
Murat V 1876	1876	Ottoman constitution announced leading to first parliament
Abdülhamit II 1876–1909	1877–78	War with Russia
	1878	Treaty of Berlin creates principality of Bulgaria and Russia acquires parts of north-eastern Anatolia
	1881	Ottoman Public Debt Office created
	1889	Ahmet Rıza founds group that later becomes Committee of Union and Progress
	1896	Violence in eastern Anatolia; Armenian Dashnaks attack the Ottoman Bank in Istanbul
	1908	'Young Turks' revolution; Bulgaria, Bosnia-Herzegovina and Crete lost by Ottomans
Mehmet V 1909–18	1909	Counter-coup: '31 March event', put down by troops from Salonica; Abdülhamit II deposed
	1912–13	Balkan Wars
	1913	CUP seizes power
	1914–18	First World War: Ottomans side with Germans
	1915	Relocation of Armenians from eastern Anatolia

	1915–16	Allied invasion and Ottoman victory at Gallipoli
Mehmet VI 1918–22	1918	Armistice signed at Mudros
	1919–22	War with Greece
	1920	Treaty of Sèvres: humiliation for Ottomans
Abdülmecit II (Caliph) 1922–24	1922	Turks defeat Greeks; Sultanate abolished, replaced by symbolic 'Caliph of all Islam'
	1923	Treaty of Lausanne establishes present-day borders of Turkey; Republic of Turkey proclaimed on 29 October with Mustafa Kemal (Atatürk) as first president
	1923–24	Turkish–Greek population exchange
	1924	Ottoman dynasty expelled; secular one-party state established; radical reforms begin
	1928	Language reform
	1938	Atatürk dies
	1952	Turkey joins NATO
	1955	Riots against Greeks in Istanbul
	1960	Military coup: prime minister Adnan Menderes hanged
	1980	Military coup
	1983	Turgut Özal's Motherland party wins elections, economy revives
	2005	Turkey begins talks on joining European Union

FURTHER READING

This is an enormous subject, with complicated clashes all over the place. Maybe the first step is to establish the worldwide context and for this there is an obvious way forward: John Darwin's *After Tamerlane: The Rise and Fall of Global Empires, 1400–2000* (London, 2008). The Ottoman Empire itself is best approached, first time round, through books with panache, and a leading one is Philip Mansel, *Constantinople: City of the World's Desire, 1453–1924* (London, 1997). A much older book, first published in 1964 yet somehow still giving an excellent introduction, is Lord (or Patrick) Kinross, *Atatürk: The Rebirth of a Nation* (London, 1993). His *The Ottoman Empire* (second edition, London, 2003) is old-fashioned, well-presented military history for the greater part, but covers the entire subject chronologically and with verve. Robert Irwin, *For Lust of Knowing: The Orientalists and their Enemies* (London, 2006) is indispensable as to the study of 'the Orient' in the West, in itself a most curious story, eccentrics all around.

From time to time enterprising publishers produce miniatures that reveal a far wider picture. Irfan Orga, *Portrait of a Turkish Family* (new edition, London, 2002) was a bestseller in the 1950s. Shirin Devrim, *A Turkish Tapestry: The Shakirs of Istanbul* (London, 1996) is an account by an aristocratic lady who became an actress in New York. Over the centuries, there have been many such revealing miniatures, two of them, at least, classics of literature. In 2007 Penguin published extracts from the letters of Lady Mary Wortley Montagu, *Life on the Golden Horn*, and see Helmuth von Moltke, *Unter dem Halbmond: Erlebnisse in der alten Türkei 1835–1839*

(Stuttgart, 1984). Brian Sewell, *South from Ephesus: An Escape from the Tyranny of Western Art* (London, 2002) is a modern such miniature. The largest collection of such books is that of Ömer Koç, a two-volume catalogue of which is in preparation. A very deserving Istanbul publisher, Sinan Kuneralp of ISIS, has for years been reprinting hundreds of the outstanding old period pieces, in the main western languages (such as the memoirs of the British ambassador in 1878, Austen Henry Layard). The ISIS catalogue is again to be consulted. There are many very good books on Istanbul and I shall here cite just one. Hilary Sumner-Boyd and John Freely, *Strolling Through Istanbul: The Classic Guide to the City* (revised edition, London, 2010) takes you round, but you will need stout shoes. Robert Irwin, *Islamic Art* (London, 1997) explains much else.

There have been several attempts at a short, readable history, of which we might single out Jason Goodwin, *Lords of the Horizons: A History of the Ottoman Empire* (London, 1998) and Dimitri Kitsikis, *L'Empire ottoman* (Paris, 1985) which is extremely thoughtful as to the Greek-Turkish relationship. Justin McCarthy, *The Ottoman Turks: An Introductory History to 1923* (London, 1997) is a bravely scholarly attempt, not shrinking from the economic side.

There is, nowadays, as archival access is easier (not least via the Internet), a small flood of academic studies of this or that aspect of the empire's history, many of them written in English by Turks themselves. Some of these can be hard work even for specialists; according to the Nestor of Turkish historians, Halil İnalcık, it takes the best American graduates two years before they can comfortably read a page, but for those who triumph over the obstacles, the contribution of these scholars has sometimes been astonishing. I cannot possibly list all these, and will only cite as an instance, Gábor Ágoston, *Guns for the Sultan: Military Power and the Weapons Industry in the Ottoman Empire* (Cambridge, 2005).

The only way to reach this level of monographic enquiry is through the encyclopaedic and multi-volume scholarly works. Of these, there are several (and they sometimes repeat each other). In terms of elegance and erudition my immediate recommendation is Robert Mantran (ed.), *Histoire de l'empire ottoman* (Paris, 1989), which includes penetrating chapters by Gilles Veinstein. The book gives commendable space to the Arab provinces (including Egypt) and is especially useful for the later period, after Küçük Kaynarca. On the Young Turks it is superb. The Cambridge *An Economic and Social History of the Ottoman Empire 1300–1914,* edited by Halil İnalcık with Donald Quataert (1994), is encyclopaedic with all of the advantages and disadvantages that this implies. İnalcık himself produced a shorter *The Ottoman Empire: The Classical Age 1300–1600* (second edition, London, 2000) which is both thorough, in the sense that it deals firmly with land holding, international trade, finance, etc., and readable, and also well organized. There are comparable books by Colin Imber, *The Ottoman Empire 1300–1600: The Structure of Power* (Basingstoke, 2002) and Norman Itzkowitz, *Ottoman Empire and Islamic Tradition* (second edition, Chicago, 1980).

Turkish scholarship is on display (in English) in Ekmeleddin İhsanoğlu, *History of the Ottoman State, Society and Civilization* (2 vols, Istanbul, 2001–2). There is a wonderful *Istanbul Ansiklopedisi* (8 vols, Istanbul, 1993–95) to which I owe a great deal. Stefanos Yerasimos's thesis for the University of Paris, 'Turquie: le processus d'un sous-développement', published in Turkey as *Azgelişmişlik sürecinde Türkiye* (Istanbul, 1974), belongs to its era, when it was possible to blame underdevelopment upon imperialism, and it contains much material (including the original statement of the *Tanzimat*). Good histories of the non-Anatolian parts of the empire are L. S. Stavrianos, *The Balkans since 1453* (new edition, London, 2000) and Albert Hourani, *A History of the Arab Peoples* (London, 1991). The grand history of the Anatolian Turks in modern times is the astonishingly durable Bernard Lewis, *The Emergence of Modern Turkey*, first published in 1961 and now in its third edition (Oxford, 2002).

My own chapters have been partly based on the above books, but for each separate chapter, other references follow. I concentrate on works produced in the past ten or so years.

Prelude

Fritz Neumark, *Zuflucht am Bosporus: deutsche Gelehrte, Politiker und Künstler in der Emigration, 1933–1953* (Frankfurt, 1980) is the outstanding memoir, and Horst Widmann, *Exil und Bildungshilfe: Die deutschsprachige Emigration in die Türkei nach 1933* (Frankfurt, 1973) is an admirable account. There was also an exhibition at the Akademie der Künste in Berlin in 2000. Its catalogue, edited by Sabine Hillebrecht, *Haymatloz: Exil in der Türkei 1933–1945* is splendid. Arnold Reisman, *Turkey's Modernization: Refugees from Nazism and Atatürk's Vision* (Washington, DC, 2006) is the main English-language account. For Hikmet, see *The Poems of Nazim Hikmet*, translated by Randy Blasing and Mutlu Konuk (second edition, New York, 2002).

Chapters 1–8

There are many books on the Central Asian Mongol-Tatar-Turkish horse-archer empires. The warhorse is René Grousset, *The Empire of the Steppes: A History of Central Asia* (New Brunswick, NJ, 1970) but I have a great weakness for Jean-Paul Roux, *Histoire des Turcs: deux mille ans du Pacifique à la Méditerranée* (second edition, Paris, 2000), but his conclusions as to proper names (e.g. Kirghiz) are challenged. Study of what the Russian Lev Gumilev called 'the ancient Turks' is exceedingly difficult and there are scholarly hostilities involved, which I am not competent to arbitrate. As to the Tatar-Turkish-Russian relationship, a speculative essay is Norman Stone, 'Turkey in the Russian Mirror' in Ljubica Erickson and Mark Erickson (eds), *Russia: War, Peace and Diplomacy. Essays in honour of John Erickson* (London, 2004).

On the language, the outstanding description is Geoffrey Lewis, *Turkish Grammar* (second edition, Oxford, 2000). The most useful primer

I know is A. and D. Pollard, *Teach Yourself Turkish* (new edition, London, 2003). It does not treat you as if you were a baby.

Heath W. Lowry, *The Nature of the Early Ottoman State* (Albany, NY, 2003) is well written and much challenged. Cemal Kafadar, *Between Two Worlds: The Construction of the Ottoman State* (Berkeley, 1995) is useful for the background. For the collapse of Byzantium, the latest scholarly work is Nevra Necipoğlu, *Byzantium between the Ottomans and the Latins: Politics and Society in the Late Empire* (Cambridge, 2009) though Speros Vryonis, *The Decline of Medieval Hellenism in Asia Minor: And the Process of Islamization from the Eleventh through the Fifteenth Century* (new edition, Berkeley, 1986) is *the* elegiac Greek book. But Edward Gibbon, who cannot wait for 1453, may be endlessly re-read: *The History of the Decline and Fall of the Roman Empire*, edited by David Womersley (6 vols, London, 1997).

The outstanding book on 1453 is Roger Crowley, *Constantinople: The Last Great Siege* (London, 2005), endlessly interesting on the technicalities.

On the period 1453–1774 I will add the following to the general accounts above. Steven Runciman, *The Great Church in Captivity* (new edition, Cambridge, 1985) is a superb performance and I know no better explanation of the theological differences of Latin and Orthodox. Noel Malcolm, *Bosnia: A Short History* (London, 1994) and *Kosovo: A Short History* (London, 1998) examine the Ottoman presence in the Balkans with extraordinary erudition. John Freely, *Jem Sultan: Adventures of a Captive Turkish Prince in Renaissance Europe* (London, 2004) reveals much as to the Mediterranean background, and Roger Crowley, *Empires of the Sea: The Final Battle for the Mediterranean 1521–1580* (London, 2008) shows the same qualities as his earlier book on 1453. Another Istanbul resident, Geoffrey Goodwin, wrote entertainingly on *The Janissaries* (London, 1994) and on *Topkapı Palace* (London, 1999) but there is a magnificent catalogue also, *Topkapı à Versailles: trésors de la cour ottomane* (Paris, 1999). Caroline Finkel, *Osman's Dream: The Story of the Ottoman Empire 1300–1923* (London, 2005) gives a sound exposition of the Shia-Safavid problem, and she is indispensable for the much understudied eighteenth century. The latest work on the siege of Vienna and its context is Andrew Wheatcroft, *The Enemy at the Gate: Habsburgs, Ottomans and the Battle for Europe* (London, 2008), the advantage of which is the author's deep knowledge of the Austrian army and the military frontier.

For the century between Küçük Kaynarca and the Congress of Berlin, the international context is explained in Tim Blanning's multifaceted *The Pursuit of Glory: Europe 1648–1815* (London, 2007). Since Albert Sorel's more than century-old *L'Europe et la Révolution Française* there has not been a better explanation as to how the Eastern Question developed. Orlando Figes's *Crimea: The Last Crusade* (London, 2010) is the latest, there. On the internationalization of Ottoman questions, there is a depressing book on the Lebanon: Leila Tarazi Fawaz, *An Occasion for War: Civil Conflict in Lebanon and Damascus in 1860* (London, 1994). There are good Turkish books on the collapse of finances, such as Haydar Kazgan, *Osmanlıda Avrupa Finans Kapitali* (Istanbul, 1995), but David S. Landes, *Bankers and Pashas: International Finance and Economic Imperialism in Egypt* (Cambridge, Mass, 1980) is a considerable work, distinguished by sympathy for the Egyptians and Turks who were gulled. On the pre-Fukuyama atmosphere of the 1860s in general, see Norman Stone, *Europe Transformed 1878–1919* (second edition, Oxford, 1999). Mark Bostridge, *Florence Nightingale: The Woman and Her Legend* (London, 2008) is a noble portrait of a noble woman.

Emre Aracı, *Donizetti Paşa* (Istanbul, 2006) opens the interesting artery of Turco-Western music. Stéphane (*sic*) Yerasimos has some penetrating thoughts in *Hommes et idées dans l'espace ottoman* (Istanbul, 1997), and I had not quite understood, before reading his essay, 'A propos des réformes urbaines des Tanzimat' (pp. 305–19), why Islamic towns are so very different from Christian ones. Edhem Eldem, Daniel Goffman and Bruce Masters, *The Ottoman City between East and West: Aleppo, Izmir and Istanbul* (Cambridge, 2008) greatly expands the point.

As regards the empire's last forty years, we are in flux as the archives open and the era is reconsidered. In the last twelve years or so, there has been serious reappraisal of Abdülhamit II, as with Selim Deringil, *The Well-Protected Domains: Ideology and the Legitimation of Power in the Ottoman Empire, 1876–1909* (London, 1998) and François Georgeon, *Abdülhamid II* (Paris, 2003). The chief book on the floods of refugees from the mid-nineteenth century onwards is Justin McCarthy, *Death and Exile: The Ethnic Cleansing of Ottoman Muslims, 1821–1922* (Princeton, 1996) but compare Oliver Bullough, *Let Our Fame be Great: Journeys among the Defiant People of the Caucasus* (London, 2010). On the opposition, the classic is Niyazi Berkes, *The Development of Secularism in Turkey* (London, 1998) but Şerif Mardin, *Religion, Society and Modernity in Turkey* (Syracuse, NY, 2006) and M. Şükrü Hanıoğlu, *A Brief History of the Late Ottoman Empire* (Princeton, 2008) are important. Sina Akşin, *Jön Türkler ve İttihat ve Terakki* (third edition, Istanbul, 2001) gives an important link between the Young Turks and the Committee. Another important book is Fuat Dündar, *Modern Türkiye'nin şifresi* (Istanbul, 2008) although it overrates the degree to which Talât, overwhelmed by refugees from the Balkan Wars, would be thinking of Professor Durkheim. Mark Mazower, *Salonica, City of Ghosts: Christians, Muslims and Jews* (New York, 2005) is particularly good on the disintegration period, and Trotsky, *The Balkan Wars, 1912–1913: The War Correspondence of Leon Trotsky* (New York, 1980), edited by George Weissman and Duncan Williams, could write a paragraph. Since we are in warhorse country, it is remarkable that A. J. P. Taylor's *The Struggle for Mastery in Europe 1848–1918*, first published in 1954, remains extremely useful for the Balkan Wars.

On the background to war in 1914, Norman Stone, *World War One: A Short History* (London, 2007) rediscovers the Turkish background, spelled out in Mustafa Aksakal, *The Ottoman Road to War in 1914* (Cambridge, 2008). The war itself has received a monumental treatment by Stanford J. Shaw, *The Ottoman Empire in World War I* (2 vols, Ankara, 2006). He deals at length with the Armenian disaster, and regards it as a disaster rather than as a genocide, as if to the people on the ground this made much difference. The best recent account of the Armenian massacres is Guenter Lewy, *The Armenian Massacres in Ottoman Turkey: A Disputed Genocide* (Salt Lake City, 2005). Franz Werfel's famous novel, *The Forty Days of Musa Dagh* (London, 1934) has that readable-in-a-night quality, but he himself wrote on the manuscript, 'do not use this against the Turks', because he knew that there were complications and understood what the Turkish Republic was managing to do. Roderic H. Davison, *Essays in Ottoman and Turkish History, 1774–1923: The Impact of the West* (Austin, TX, 1990) has an important article on this, and compare Elie Kedourie (with an introduction by David Pryce-Jones), *The Chatham House Version and Other Middle Eastern Studies* (Chicago, 2004). It matters because it explodes the notion of Armenian innocence.

On Gallipoli the established British book is Nigel Steel and Peter Hart, *Defeat at Gallipoli* (London, 1994) but Kevin Fewster, Vecihi Basarin and Hatice Hurmuz Basarin, *Gallipoli: The Turkish Story* (Sydney, 2003) should be noted.

On the emergence of a new order in the Middle East after 1918, David Fromkin, *A Peace to End All Peace: Creating the Modern Middle East, 1914–1922* (London, 1989) has established itself deservedly as *the* book that everyone reads. On the Turkish side, Stanford J. Shaw, *From Empire to Republic: The Turkish War of National Liberation, 1918–1923* (5 vols, Ankara, 2000) is now the standard account but Michael Llewellyn Smith, *Ionian Vision: Greece in Asia Minor, 1919–1922* (second edition, London, 1998) is in every way a distinguished book, fair minded and scholarly. The best recent short account, missing out nothing essential, is Andrew Mango, *From the Sultan to Atatürk: Turkey* (London, 2009).

Epilogue: The Turkish Republic

Andrew Mango, *Atatürk* (London, 2004) is the obvious place to start, the more so as it links the pre-1923 period with the later one. Kemal H. Karpat has written so extensively on this, and for that matter on detailed day-to-day developments, that I am tempted to suggest just an Internet search. His book on *Social Change and Politics in Turkey: A Structural-Historical Analysis* (Leiden, 1973) builds on a lifetime effort, with extraordinarily interesting results in various domains, to synthesize democracy, nationalism and Islam. The contradictions are such that, to an extraordinary extent, modern-day Turks have left their ultra-modern history to foreigners. Single episodes, yes, and in the case of Mete Tunçay, writing on the one-party regime of the 1930s, distinguishedly so. But the world could do with an authoritative account by a native Turk. Andrew Mango's own *The Turks Today* (London, 2004) is an efficient and well-documented survey, and William Hale wrote the authoritative account, *Turkish Politics and the Military* (London, 1994). The outstanding book on Kurdish matters is, in my opinion, Hamit Bozarslan, *La Question kurde: états et minorités au Moyen-Orient* (Paris, 1997) though there are many others. Its strength lies in its lack of self-pity.

Geoffrey Lewis was the world leader on the Turkish languages and *The Turkish Language Reform: A Catastrophic Success* (Oxford, 1999) shows this great man in all his glory, betimes with shouts of laughter.

Journalists have sometimes been very good, provided that they stayed long enough. David Hotham, *The Turks* (London, 1972) is followed by Nicole and Hugh Pope, *Turkey Unveiled: Atatürk and After* (London, 1997) which foresaw, and sympathized with, the rise of an Islamic version of Christian Democracy and otherwise understood that the period of the 1980s had had a great many positive sides to it. Francis Russell, *Places in Turkey: A Pocket Grand Tour* (London, 2010) is a *tour de force*, describing fascinating and often relatively unknown places. But there is, so to speak, eternal Turkey, and how people live. Geert Mak, *The Bridge: A Journey Between Orient and Occident* (London, 2008) describes badly paid fourteen-hour huckstering work on the Galata Bridge, with enormous detail as to how people conduct their lives in those circumstances. A genius.

LIST OF ILLUSTRATIONS

INDEX